Pael, ~~~~~~
714/6867495
W9-CZL-520

Spiritual Warfare

*A Guide to Controlling the Mind
and the Emotions*

by
John A. Jackson

authorHOUSE™

1663 LIBERTY DRIVE, SUITE 200
BLOOMINGTON, INDIANA 47403
(800) 839-8640
WWW.AUTHORHOUSE.COM

This book is a work of non-fiction. Unless otherwise noted, the author and the publisher make no explicit guarantees as to the accuracy of the information contained in this book and in some cases, names of people and places have been altered to protect their privacy.

© 2005 John Jackson. All Rights Reserved.

No part of this book may be reproduced, stored in a retrieval system, or transmitted by any means without the written permission of the author.

First published by AuthorHouse 07/26/05

ISBN: 1-4208-5622-7 (sc)

Library of Congress Control Number: 2005904143

Printed in the United States of America
Bloomington, Indiana

This book is printed on acid-free paper.

Contents

Introduction   vii

Foreword   ix

Chapter 1 – The Basis for Self Acceptance   1

Chapter 2 – A Principle for Controlling the Emotions   21

Chapter 3 – The Principle of Renewing the Mind   37

Chapter 4 – Depression, Emotional Self-Centeredness   51

Chapter 5 – The Key to Controlling Resentment   67

Chapter 6 – Control Anger, Become A Grace Giver   87

Chapter 7 – A Parable on Uncontrolled Emotions   103

Chapter 8 – The Futility in Anxiety   117

Chapter 9 – Unholy Fear Under Control   131

Chapter 10 – A Spiritual Response to Emotional Problems   145

Chapter 11 – Rejecting Feelings of Rejection & Overcoming Guilt   159

Chapter 12 – How to Destroy Strongholds   175

Chapter 13 – Preparation for Spiritual Warfare   193

Chapter 14 – The Final Battle Plan-prayer   209

Introduction

Do you struggle with your emotions? Have you ever felt strapped into an out-of-control roller coaster ride of turbulent reactions? Are you sometimes driven by feelings you know are sinful and harmful? Everyone has encountered the battle of the emotions. Perhaps you can relate to the turmoil in the Jones's household. It is almost time for Joe to come home from work. Ann wants everything to be just right tonight, so she's setting the table with extra care, using her best china. She can smell the delicate flavors of Joe's favorite meal bubbling in the oven. She places the plates just so in the center of the placemats. But she feels a little frustrated because her day has been stressful. Her elementary-age daughter, Michelle, has been banished to her bedroom for kicking her little brother, Benny. Ann can hear Michelle angrily screaming from behind the door. "You be quiet in there!" Ann yells as she folds napkins and sets them neatly beside the plates. The screams continue without a break, so Ann threatens, "You'd better stop screaming or I'm going to take away your bike for a week!" The screaming still continues, so Ann keeps threatening. Benny, who was playing in the living room, tunes out his mother's voice and wanders outside to ride his tricycle. As he pedals across the driveway, he notices a ball laying in the yard. He abandons his trike to play with the ball.

A few minutes later, Joe's sedan screeches to a stop in the driveway. His front bumper barely misses crushing the front tire of the little red trike. Joe shoves open the door, his face red with irritation. "Ann," he hollers, "get out here and get this pile of junk out of the driveway! When I come home, I'm tired and I don't want the children's toys in my way!" Ann's head pops out of the front screen door. She speaks in a slow, controlled voice, "Joe, I have told you a thousand times to keep your voice down! What will the neighbors think?" Joe jumps out of his car, tosses the trike onto the lawn, then pulls his car fully into the driveway. As soon as he closes the front door, Ann says, "Wash up for dinner right away. I've fixed your favorite meal." Then she walks down the hall to tell Michelle she can come to the dinner table. As soon as Michelle reaches the kitchen, she starts howling, "I'm hungry. I wanna eat!"

When everyone is seated, Benny immediately grabs a muffin from a basket in the center of the table and crams it into his mouth. "Put it back, Benny," Ann insists. "I want your father to thank God for the food first. That is if he's grateful for all the work I've gone to. Are you, Joe?" she demands in a grating voice. "Oh, shut up!" Joe responds. "All I want is a little peace and respect around here. But all you do is nag at everything I do. For once, let's eat our dinner in peace." Joe pours gravy over his mashed potatoes and roast beef. He scoops up a generous portion of potatoes with his fork and shoves it into his mouth. Before he completely finishes swallowing, he grimaces. "For crying out loud! Can't you ever handle the saltshaker gently? You've put so much salt in this gravy that it tastes like it's made out of sea water." A lump forms in Ann's throat and tears fill her eyes. Her beautifully set table seems to have lost its shine and the children stare at their plates without a word. Joe hardly notices when Ann puts down her napkin and retreats to the bedroom.

This scene is like those we experience at one time or another. If you asked them, neither Joe nor Ann would say that their purpose was to hurt each other. They want to build a happy marriage with loving children. But they do what they don't want to do because their emotions are out of control. The reason for this book is to assist a Christian in controlling the emotions and not allow the forces of evil to have victory. Each one of the chapters is vital in learning this lesson of being a mature Christian. The first chapter deals with the basis for controlling the emotions. It is called the basis for self-acceptance. The second chapter involves the principle for controlling the emotional man. The other chapters deal with renewing the mind, controlling depression, fear, resentment, anger, and other emotions. Chapter seven uses the parable of the prodical son to illustrate the need for the renewal of the mind and adopting the attitude of forgiveness.

The title of this book indicates it deals with spiritual warfare. Seldom would Christians debate the existence of angels; yet they are leery of saying there are demonic spirits. Spiritual warfare is defending oneself from the attack of the demonic forces. This attack usually comes through the soul rather than the flesh. The soul is the mind, will, and emotions. It is my intention to assist any Christian in resisting the devil.

In each chapter you will find an introduction, an exhortation, an opportunity to verbally communicate to the Lord, thought provoking questions, a warfare prayer starter and steps of actions. This is a practical book, which will assist you in walking with the Lord. You will find that warfare prayers will place an emphasis of reviewing the past and an awareness of past events has power over ones life.

The basis for renewing the mind is a passage in 2 Corinthians 10:3-5. Hypnosis is the worlds' substitute for the work of the Holy Spirit.

Foreword

I recommend the man as I recommend his work. John Jackson's work reflects a life and ministry in walking in cutting-edge truth. While the title of the book is <u>Spiritual Warfare</u>, the thrust of its message is on spiritual health. Nothing is more strategic in spiritual warfare than warriors who are healthy in spirit, soul and body.

This is a book of scriptural accuracy as well as balance. It does not give the enemy undue attention and focuses on developing mental and spiritual health as a preventative to demonic opportunity.

I have known John Jackson for a quarter of a century and have observed his boldness to pursue the fullness of God even (and especially) when it costs acceptance among those who choose the religious comfort zone. He has not been afraid to choose the desperate needs of people over religious safety. I remember when it was not "cool" to call a demon a demon and deal with demons, a most provocative stance among evangelicals, but necessary.

This study handily lends itself to personal study, group study or sermon series preparation. I pray for a wide acceptance of this carefully prepared work from the heart and pen of John Jackson.

Jack Taylor
Dimensions Ministries
Melbourne, FL

Chapter 1

જ

The Basis for Self Acceptance
Romans 8:28; 9:19-21

The following are a few questions, which need to be answered before a believer begins this study. Be honest and answer each question without attempting to determine what God would have you write.

1. If you could be anyone in the world, who would you be?

2. There are things you cannot change, but suppose you had the power to change them, what would you change?

3. Suppose you had the power to change a situation, what would you change?

4. If you had the power to change a relationship or another person, what would you do?

5. Do you accept your family as God's perfect gift to you?

Introduction

The key to controlling your emotion is found in this first chapter. This is the reason it is introduced first. As the title suggests it is **basic** for the control of most, if not all of the emotions. When a believer fully accepts himself in a manner as illustrated in this exposition, he can effectively deal with emotions, which are out of control. This is not an exposition on self-esteem. The world's view of self is entirely different from God's view. This is an exposition on seeing your self from God's perspective. Men from the beginning of time have resisted the acceptance of themselves. Eve was tempted by the devil and the temptation was to become like God. Eve was not satisfied with her limitations and wanted to be like God. By succumbing to the temptation she revealed a desire to be more than what God created. This was Satan's first temptation aimed at the emotions. The question could be asked, "Why does a failure to accept myself the way God has created me, affect my emotions?" The answer to this question will be explained in this chapter. To reject oneself is a rejection of the will and purpose of God.

In chapter nine of Romans, Paul has illustrated the sovereignty of God. God chooses those to whom He will show mercy and compassion. His wisdom and will are an expression of His sovereignty. Indeed, He is the Creator of all things. Most Christians accept and acknowledge mentally, God's absolute sovereignty. They accept His attributes of being all knowing, all-powerful, etc. However, there is a distinct difference in knowing and acknowledging something as true and accepting it by faith with one's heart. It is easier to accept God's sovereignty over the problems of others, than His sovereignty over your personal problems. Someone may ask, **"How does accepting one's self affect a believer in controlling the emotions?"** Anyone who cannot accept God's plan and purpose for his life is practicing rebellion against God. As the title of this exposition suggests, the acceptance of self is basic for a believer to control his emotions. Many emotional conflicts root into a rejection of self. This is amplified in chapter ten. If a believer cannot say, "I accept myself as God has created me, and I thank God that I am who I am," he is resisting God as Creator.

> *Text: "You will say to me then, 'Why does He, still find fault? For who resists His will?' On the contrary, who are you, O man, who answers back to God? The thing molded will not say to the molder, 'Why did you make me like this,' will it? Or does not the potter have a right over the clay, to make from the same lump one vessel for honorable use, and another for common use?'' Romans 9:19-21 "And we know that God causes all things to work together for good to those who love God, to those who are called according to His purpose." Romans 8:28.*

These passages reveal the age-old idea I would like to be more than who I think I am. This was Eve's problem and it has been the problem with mankind ever since. Thinking and acting in this manner in effect shows a desire to be God. This passage indicates a believer is to accept God's creation by faith and thank Him for creating us.

The Facts About God's Sovereignty

We will first review the sovereignty of God. **He is a God who does all things. He is a God who has the right to do all things. He is a God who does all things right**.

HE IS A GOD WHO DOES ALL THINGS

God is in charge of this universe. Despite what evolutionists teach, He is the Creator. John in his gospel wrote, "*All Things came into being by Him and apart from Him nothing came into being that has come into being.*" John 1:3. Paul wrote in Colossians 1:16-18, "*For by Him all thing were created, both in the heavens and on earth, visible and invisible, whether thrones or dominions or rulers or authorities-all things have been created by Him and for Him.*" John also wrote in the book of Revelation, "*Worthy art Thou, our Lord and our God, to receive glory and honor and power, for Thou didst create all things, and because of Thy will they existed and were created.*" Revelation 4:11. To accept Him as Creator, is to accept that He has created all things including man. This means creation did not happen by chance, but was a divine plan. Since God is the Creator no birth has caught Him by surprise. Christians should accept the fact that all births are a result of His creative power and purpose. If this is true, then God knew before time to whom we would be born and when. Note what is written in the Psalms, "*For Thou didst form my inward parts; Thou didst weave me in my mother's womb.*" Psalm 139:13. Paul wrote in Ephesians, "*...just as He chose us in Him before the foundation of the world, that we should be holy and blameless before Him.*" Ephesians 1:4. Since God planned for man's salvation before He created him, it stands to reason that He knew beforehand who would be saved.

3

Real Life Illustration

In a church I pastored a marine officer attended a worship service. When I visited in his home, he informed me he was an atheist. I told him I was amazed at his faith. I indicated he had a lot more faith than me. I suggested he could believe that his television over a period of years emerged from the floor. He indicated he believed there had to be a television maker. I then said, could man make a man? He said no. I asked him if a man was more complicated than a television. He responded yes he is. I then asked about the universe and his answer was the same. I then stated the reason he had more faith than I, was because he could believe a world, universe, and man could be made without a creator. They came into existence from nothing. Two weeks later he made a decision to make the Lord his savior.

Believers know the truth of God's power and ability. However, in practice many Christians act as if God is incapable of solving life's problems. The Bible contains many passages detailing God's power and might. Isaiah and Jeremiah are quoted to illustrate this truth. *"To whom then will you liken Me that I should be his equal? Says the Holy One. Lift up your eyes on high and see who has created these stars, the One who leads forth their hosts by number, He calls them all by name; because of the greatness of his might and the strength of His power not one of them is missing." (Isaiah 40:25-26.) "Oh, Lord God! Behold thou hast made the heavens and the earth by Thy great power and by Thine outstretched arm! Nothing is too difficult for Thee."* Jeremiah 32:17. The argument that may be proposed is "God doesn't do all things." This implies that God is not in control over everything.

This question must be asked, *"What is beyond the scope of God's power and authority?"* When three angels spoke to Abraham about the possibility of Sarah having a child, the angel said, *"Is anything to difficult for the Lord?"* Our Lord is not up in heaven having deep anxiety over things which He has no control. He is Lord. Paul wrote, *"He who is the blessed and only Sovereign, the King of kings and Lord of lords; who alone possesses immortality and dwells in unapproachable light; whom no man has seen or can see."* Other questions must be answered: Does God have the power and authority to intervene in everyday problems? Are there any problems facing believers that God cannot control? Does God hear the prayers of all believers? Does God show preference to individuals who are serving in full-time ministry? Believers must accept that God is not limited, except by His own will or self-imposed restrictions or limitations.

HE IS A GOD WHO HAS A RIGHT TO DO ALL THINGS

"Or does not the potter have a right over the clay?" (Romans 9:21.) *"Right,"* in the Greek, is *exousia*, freedom of action, right to act, on authority. It is the ability or strength with which one is endued. It also includes power, authority, and the right to exercise power. Indeed, God is the potter and men are the clay. The clay has no authority over its use. The nature of clay's existence is to be used. In order to be used by a sculptor, clay must be put through a variety of processes. It must be cleansed of all impurities, mixed with other clays and put under pressure. So it is with God and man. Christians must go through trials to refine them for the potter's hand, to make whatever vessel He chooses. God will make what He wills and in accordance with His purpose. This statement by Paul alludes to a passage in Isaiah, which states, *"'Shall the potter be considered as equal with the clay, that what is made should say to its maker, 'He did not make me or what is formed say to Him who formed it, He has no understanding?'"* Isaiah 29:16.

God reveals His right through the **mystery of creation**. The doctrine of God being the creator and believers are subject to Him is best illustrated by a Man called Job. Job's problems involved financial failure, physical disabilities, emotional trauma, a loss of community esteem, a nagging wife, and a sense of spiritual deprivation. The first chapters of Job illustrate his complaining about problems. Finally the Lord asked Job, *"Who is this that darkens counsel by words without knowledge?"* Job 38:2. Job was chided because he questioned God's right or authority. God asked Job another question, which reveals this authority. *"Where were you when I laid the foundation of the earth?"* Job 38:4. Job was acting as if God could not handle his problems or was unaware of what was happening to him. God reminded Job that He had might, power, and wisdom, and that creation proved His wisdom and power. God had no need to ask any man's wisdom about His creation. He is uniquely God and operates according to His nature. The Lord was saying shut up and accept my authority.

God's response to Job also illustrates His right because of **creation's order**. The Lord questions Job about his ability to run God's creation. *"Have you ever in your life commanded the morning, and caused the dawn to know its place?"* Job 38:12. The question asked of Job and other questions like it, must be answered by those who resist the will of God. This question is only one of a series of questions, posed to Job, by God, which reveal God's authority through the order of creation. Note some of God's questions, *"Who set its measurements, since you know? Or who stretched the line on it? On what were its bases sunk? Or who laid its cornerstone? Or who enclosed the sea with doors?"* Job's answer and other believers would be "No way, could I command the morning." The following questions reveal God's power and the inabilities of man. Do you really believe God set this world in motion, and its operation is in accordance with His divine plan? Has anything occurred which has surprised God? If something did surprise God it would indicate He never anticipated the billions of people in the world. He has lost control and things are not as He planned. However, this world is functioning according to God's plan of operation. Nothing has surprised God. This validates His authority and right. For a believer to think that something occurs out of the oversight of God, demeans a Holy and sovereign God.

HE IS A GOD WHO DOES ALL THINGS RIGHT

"To make from the same lump one vessel for honorable use, and another for common use." Romans 9:21. God has not lost control of the universe. The world's growing population was always in God's plan. He is in charge of the world and everything is on target to perform His will. If God is not surprised at the increase in the population, then everything is operating according to His purpose. God does make man. Somehow some believers think they were born into the world and God had nothing to do with it. An extension of this thinking is, "My marriage was not in a church therefore, it is not sanctified by God. He had absolutely nothing to do with it." God can intervene in life and could have created any number of circumstances to halt any event. God chooses to allow things to happen and then cause them *"to work together for good."* Romans 8:28. The preceding type of thoughts progress in the believer's mind, so personal problems seems to be out of God's control.

They begin to think or live with the following expression. "When He created me He did a poor job, and if I was God I would have done things differently." God doesn't make mistakes. He is in the process of molding believers who will love, obey, and follow Him. Believers tend to compare their lot to other people including non-believers. It would be much better to walk by faith. A faith walk would indicate, I don't know what the future holds but I know who holds the future. Job is an example of this type of worldly thinking. God said to Job, "*Will the fault finder contend with the, Almighty? Let him who reproves God answer it.*" Job 40:2. "*Will you really annul My judgement? Will you condemn Me that you may be justified?*" Job 40:8. When a Christian says, things are not right in my life; it implies things are out of God's control. A person may think, "All of the circumstances which have happened, creating emotional conflict, would not have occurred if God had been on His toes." Needless to say, this is ridiculous thinking.

A second implication is, "God has a flaw in His character because He allows evil or the evil one to oppress the believer." Three books of the Bible deal with the question, why do the righteous suffer and the wicked prosper? Sometimes it does appear the god of this world is winning the battle. It is true that the righteous suffer. In the model prayer, Jesus asked the Father to "*deliver us from evil.*" Actually the word "*evil*" means *the evil one.* Believers are to be delivered from the evil one. Believers are in a war and the result must be a faith walk, believing that "*greater is He who is in me, than he who is in the world.*" God has a purpose for His children and things are functioning according to His purpose. However, there are principles God has set in motion to govern the universe. He seldom over-rides those principles, and when He does, it is known by man as a miracle. God causes all of these apparent problems to work together for good. This principle is found in Romans 8:28. "*And we know God causes, all things to work together for good to those who love God, to those who are called according to His purpose.*"

An additional implication is, "God doesn't know or cannot control the future, and today's circumstances were unforeseen and have no lasting value." Most believers would object to this statement, but in every day living they express it in varying degrees. When Christians allow a problem to rob them of their joy and peace, they are practicing disbelief in the truth that God does all things right. When a problem occupies the mind and the emotions and begins to destroy the practicing of faith, it reveals unbelief in this principle. Early in my ministry a child died while asleep. The parents blamed God, and it destroyed their fellowship with Him. The baby's death thwarted their spiritual growth until they came to accept the sovereignty of God in practical living.

A Focus on Man's Submission

THE IMPRACTICALITY OF RESISTING GOD'S WILL

Let us focus on man's submission and the impracticality of resisting God's will. *"For who resists His will?"* *"Resist"* is a combination of two words *anti*, against and *histemi*, to stand. It is in the perfect tense. It speaks of a process of *standing* against God's will, which arrives at a finished state and results in a permanent stand against God. A man may resist God's will, for a short time, but he cannot maintain resistance. The resistance is within the mind of man. God cannot be resisted. If He could be, He wouldn't be God. Christians often fail to understand the nature of God. God spoke through the prophet Isaiah saying, *"I am the Lord, and there is no other; besides Me there is no god."* Christians who love God have demeaned His name by giving more strength to His enemies than they deserve. It is good to be aware of Satan and his demonic spirits. However, to fear Satan more than the Lord is walking in unbelief.

In this verse "will" is *boulama*. Kettle states this is a rare term and denotes the will as plan, purpose, or intention. Paul's message to the Philippians revealed ultimate submission by all mankind. *"That at the name of Jesus every knee should bow, of those who are in heaven, and on earth and under the earth."* Philippians 2:10. If every knee will bow to the Lord, no one will be able to resist His will. Needless to say this act will not take place on earth. However, it doesn't make good sense to resist the will of God when ultimately you will submit to Him. This question asked by God, deserves only one answer from believers; "No one can ultimately resist His will."

However, many believers attempt to resist His will every day by the failure to accept themselves as being created according to God's purpose. Resistance to the will of God is failing to submit. A failure to submit doesn't provide the believer spiritual protection from the enemy. James wrote, *"Submit, therefore, to God and resist the devil and he will flee from you."* James 4:7. A failure to submit means a failure to resist the devil. Resisting the will of God would identify a believer as rebellious. This would encourage a satanic attack.

THE IMPOSSIBILITY OF RESISTING GOD'S WILL

It is impossibility to resist God's will. Paul wrote, *"For who resists His will?"* The emphasis is on the pronoun *who* and there is no answer to this question, since it is impossible to resist the will or purpose of God. Throughout the ages men and women have attempted to resist God's will. If one could resist the will of God, then God would be subordinate to that person. God would no longer be God. James wrote, *"God is opposed to the proud but gives grace to the humble."* James 4:6. Anytime a Christian resists the authority of God he exposes his pride. He is not acting in humility. This invites God's opposition, not His support. Most believers would say, "I would never oppose God." Yet in practice this is often the case. If believers cannot accept themselves as God creation, their attitude states the following, "If I was God, I would have created me differently." Prior to the new birth the mind was reinforced over and over with a projected attitude of selfishness. The idea of submitting to God as Creator was foreign to the mind. As a believer, these thoughts are still implanted in the subconscious and need to be dealt with in a systematic way. See the chapter on renewing the mind and how to destroy strongholds. When a Christian fails to accept life and its problems, and has a resistance to praising God for self and life, it is practicing unbelief and showing resistance to God.

Jonah the Old Testament prophet, attempted to resist the will of God. He was not in agreement with the assignment of ministry to preach to a wicked city called Nineveh and fled on a ship. God caused a storm to get the attention of Jonah. After a great fish swallowed him, he came to himself and told God he would do His will. The Lord spared his life. How can you resist the one who gives and takes life? To resist His will is to dishonor and disrespect Him as the Lord of lords and King of kings.

THE IMPLICATIONS OF RESISTING GOD'S WILL

It examines God's purpose

The implications in resisting God's will which in effect is examining God's purpose for one's life. *"Why did you make me like this?"* This question is asked by people daily including believers. Can you imagine questioning God regarding the act of creation? Some people would respond, "God didn't make me, I just happened to be born." God's unique principle of creation illustrates nothing happens by chance. To question one's creation, is in effect to say, "If I had been God, I would have made me a different person." The Lord is creator and He makes all mankind according to His purpose. Man's limited knowledge cannot fathom God's purpose for life. How can God make good come out of the hurts and injuries in life? How these problems will work out for good confounds the mind. His purpose is seldom known or seen by most believers. How can any believer examine the purpose of the creator of all mankind? With limited foresight and intelligence, it is impossible. However, many believers continue questioning the purpose of God. Anytime a believer asks why, over an extended period of time in regard to a problem, it reveals a lack of faith in God. It also reveals the inner desire for God to explain His reasons for allowing the problem to happen.

It exalts one's person

The outcome of a failure to submit is to exalt one's person. This in effect is making self a god. The thought communicated by believers by not accepting themselves is, "I know better than God what I should be." Again it is saying, "If I were God, I would change things." A finite mind can never completely understand the purposes of an infinite God. The most difficult task for a believer is to submit to the will of God in all things. It becomes difficult to thank the Lord for a scarred face, a baldhead, pimples, and a host of other maladies. Yet God is able to change any and all circumstances. However, it must be within His purpose. God knew before a person's birth, all of the so-called deformities. He could have changed them instead He allows them to build character and bring forth good. The failure to accept oneself is resisting God and is nothing less than self-exaltation. When a person thinks or acts as if they know better than God what should have happened, they have in effect committed idolatry. This attitude is making self the god of one's life.

When believers cannot accept God's purposes in life, and continually indicate changes would be made if they were in charge, it is nothing more than self-exaltation. Needless to say, this is rebellion against the authority of God. It may not be a deliberate attempt to demean God, but the result is God is not the Lord of one's life.

Real Life Illustration

Before marriage as a twenty seven year old college graduate, I had a superior, haughty attitude. This attitude was based on a failure to accept myself as a person worthy of love and acceptance by God and others. This outward superior attitude was a fancy cover-up for a timid, fearful person. The following illustrates this attitude. One Sunday evening, while in a college group, I was strutting like a peacock, and a beautiful lady said, "You think you are God's gift to women, don't you? My response was "No, but heaven only knows I have ever right to be." Isn't this a nauseating attitude? This only reveals how the inner feelings of inadequacy are covered up and a lack of self-acceptance or godly self worth.

It exposes man's rebellion

The following thoughts or expression exposes man's rebellion against God's will. "I cannot accept God's will." "I resist praising God for who I am and for life's circumstances." God sees this sort of rebellious thoughts, attitudes, and the expressed verbal feelings as a rebelling against His commands. Rebellion is described by Samuel, as the sin of witchcraft. *"For rebellion is as the sin of divination (witchcraft) and insubordination is as iniquity and idolatry."* 1 Samuel 15:23. The resistance of God's purpose or will for one's life is in effect to say to God, "You have made me and You made a mistake." Most believers would argue that a failure to accept all of life's ills and especially one's self is not rebellion. Christians acting in rebellion play into the hand of the devil. However, God is sovereign and nothing happens without His knowledge. Remember Paul said in Romans 8:28, *"And we know that God causes all things to work together for good to those who love God, to those who are called according to His purpose."* What is to be excluded in *all things*? Can He really make all things work together for good? If the answer is yes, then to resent life's problems is to resent God. To resent God is a silent rejection of His person and purpose.

A Faith in God's Sovereignty

A FAITH WHICH ACKNOWLEDGES GOD'S PERSON

What is being asked of a believer is to have faith in God's sovereignty. Faith acknowledges God's person and purpose. In the face of troubles and trials to say that God will indeed cause these to work for good, requires faith. Faith according to Hebrews 11:1 is defined as *"Now faith is the assurance of things hoped for, the conviction of things not seen."* Hope is used in the Bible as guaranteed assurance. Therefore, a believer has the assurance of a guaranteed assurance. It is evidence of things not seen. One can exercise faith on the basis of God's guaranteed assurance. He has given that assurance in Romans 8:28. Let us examine Hebrews 11:1 In the KJV the passage states, *"Faith is the substance of things hoped for and the evidence of things not yet seen."* In essence substance can be seen but hope indicates it cannot be seen. The same applies with evidence it can be seen yet the passage indicates it is not seen. A practical definition of faith is, to believe you have something when you don't have it, in order to receive it. It is a belief something is so, when it doesn't appear to be so in order for it to be so. This means to accept the fact God will cause all things to work together for a believer's good, when it appears it is impossible. This is faith on the basis of His word. By the way, if it were not impossible for man, then it would not require faith. Faith believes the impossible, possible and faith comes through the word of God.

Faith demands that a Christian say, "I accept myself as God has created me. My emotions are screaming a different story. However, I refuse to allow my emotions to dictate my reaction to God. I declare by faith, His sovereign power over me. I will continue affirming the acceptance of myself many times a day, until my emotions come into harmony with what God says is true." A Christian may say, "I cannot make this statement if I don't feel like it. I would be lying. The truth is God said it is true and your emotions are lying. Act from the level of the spirit, not from the level of the soul. This is the reason it takes faith. Paul wrote, *"...who answers back to God?"* It is essential to accept the word of God over your will, mind, and emotions.

The opposite of resisting the will of God is accepting His will. Accepting God's will is submission, which requires an act and attitude of faith. "Answers back" in the Greek is *antapokrinomai*, a combination of anti, against and apokrinomai to answer. It is in effect, to question or even sass God as Creator. Can you imagine a believer expressing this attitude toward the Lord? Note what the apostle John wrote about the Lord, "*...and on His robe and on His thigh, He has a name written, King of kings, and Lord of lords.*" Revelation 19:16. God is infinite man is finite. Man must accept God as a God of wisdom and of love. Not to acknowledge Him in this way is to declare Him incompetent.

Paul wrote, "*He who is the blessed and only Sovereign, the King of kings and Lord of lords; who alone possesses immortality and dwells in inapproachable light, whom no man has seen or can see. To Him be honor and eternal dominion, amen.*" I Timothy 6:15-16. To express faith in God's person and purpose trusts Him in the midst of problems and difficulties. A failure to accept oneself is answering back to God, Why did You make me like this? The thing molded will not say to the molder, "Why did you make me like this?" The Greek word for molded is *plasma* which is anything molded or shaped into a form. The word was used to describe an artist or molder of clay, which molded clay or wax into a form. The clay should have no resistance to the hands of the master potter.

The acceptance of God's will require a believer to accept self. A Christian must be able to say, "If I had a choice of being anyone in the world, I would choose to be me. If I had the power to change myself, I would not change myself in any way. For God does have that power and He has chosen me to be the way I am. I am God's creation and He purposed me to be who I am. I thank Him I am who I am." The failure to accept oneself in this manner is to say, "God made a mistake in the act of creation." It also shows disbelief in God's ability to bring good out of what appears bad. In asking the question "Would you change yourself if you had the power?" Many believers would answer the question with a yes. The question is, "Does God have the power to change a person?" Since He does, why did God not change things? Some believers will say, "I don't want to be rebellious against God, but I cannot accept myself or this problem. I do not believe my failure to accept myself or this problem is rebellion." This kind of statement is a fleshly attitude of doubt that God is in charge of a believer's total life. A believer's desire not to be rebellious does not keep one from displaying an attitude of rebellion. Resentment of life's trials and problems is rebellion against God.

A FAITH WHICH ACKNOWLEDGES GOD'S PURPOSE

An acceptance of God's creative purpose is prompted by faith and usually requires acting in faith. Many believers can accept themselves, but have difficulty accepting others and life's circumstances. Every believer should be able to accept his or her mother and father, wife or husband, son or daughter. This is difficult because many relatives have physically and emotionally abused Christians. They have difficulty forgiving; much less believing God can cause these difficulties to work together for good. Can you say, "If I had to choose any mate in the world, I would choose the one to whom I am married?" God did have that choice, and He permitted this marriage to occur. **Faith believes the impossible**. Faith is to accept life's circumstances as under the permissive will of God and nothing happens without His knowledge. He can change any circumstance, but prefers to allow His divine principles to govern the world. These principles operate automatically, and He has to perform a miracle to change things.

A husband may say, "My wife drives me up the wall with her constant nagging." The truth is God is allowing this weakness in the wife to reveal a weakness in the husband. When the husband deals with his problem, then God will alleviate the irritation. Life's irritations are God's finger pointing out a weakness. When that weakness is dealt with, there is no reason for the irritation, unless it is to teach patience. An old adage is, "They have jumped from the frying pan into the fire." This adage indicates God will correct His children even if it means placing them into more difficult problems. The end result is to bring His children into spiritual maturity, so the end justifies the means. It is imperative for believers to accept life's irritations as the finger of God pointing out spiritual weaknesses, which need to be corrected. It has been said the irritations of life are nothing more than God's heavenly sandpaper sanding down a Christians rough spots. Many believers believe God allows life irritations as a punishment for sin. He is a loving God and wants a believer to have life and have it more abundantly. John 10:10. Life's problems are allowed in order for believers to have an abundant life.

Real Life Illustration

I taught this principle in marriage classes for years. When the children were small and had gone to bed, my wife left the water running while brushing her teeth. Since the lavatory was in our bedroom, and the children were asleep, we had the TV turned down low. I strained to listen to the sport's report on the late news. On numerous occasions I had asked her not to brush her teeth during the sport's report. As I was growing more irritated, the Lord seemed to speak to my spirit saying, "John do you love sports more than Lena?" I immediately thought, "No I don't." Then the Lord seemed to say, "Then why do you get irritated when she brushes her teeth during a sports report?" My response was, "You are right Lord, and I am acting as if I love sports more than Lena. However, this is not the case and I will never complain or resent this action in the future, for I do love her more than any sport." I then made a commitment not to complain again about Lena brushing her teeth during the sports report. To my knowledge this never occurred again, although more than likely it did. God allowed the irritation to deal with me, and when He accomplished His purpose the irritation was gone. When God gets a Christian's attention through irritations and the weakness is corrected, the irritation usually is removed.

The tendency for most believers is to say, "I believe the Bible is God's word and that it is relevant to meet any need of today." This holds true until this truth is applied to their particular problem. If the Lord can *cause all things to work together for good*, why does a believer resent problems or those who bring these problems about? Why is there such a problem in forgiving the offences of others? It is one thing to say I accept the word of God and another to practically apply it in everyday living. To accept God's word is to apply it to all matters. This application is to praise and thank God for all of life's irritations and difficulties. **A failure to praise God in the midst of all things is a practice of unbelief**. As was mentioned in the first part of this exposition, this is the key to spiritual growth. The acceptance of God as the potter and self as the result of his molding is basic to accepting other principles. This principle of accepting yourself, as God's creative act, must be exercised by faith. Faith believes something is so, when it doesn't feel like it is so, so it may be so.

Real Life Illustration

I was raised in a poor rural setting. Being small for my age, I was picked on at school. As a result of this and many other things, I grew up hating myself. I had the tendency to be a loner. As a teenager this hatred for self intensified. When I became an adult I would avoid eye contact when I looked in a mirror. This hatred of self was shown in a hot temper and a superiority complex. It was difficult to trust God and love Him. As a believer, I did not think God would love me as much as others or even answer my prayers. I had a deep resentment for my person. My first gift, as a pastor of a congregation, was given to my children and I could not use it for myself. As a result of reading and studying the Bible and hearing the testimony of others, I began applying this principle of accepting self. This truth changed my concept of self and of God. In order to change my attitude toward self, I would look into a mirror. I would make eye contact and say, "I am a person of worth and value. God loves me and I accept myself as God's perfect gift to myself. I thank God that I am, who I am." This was repeated a number of times each day. I continued in this manner for months. This resulted in an acceptance of self and of God as Creator. It also helped develop me in becoming a mature believer trusting God for everything and in everything.

Verbal Commitment to the Lord

Repeat the following to another person or to the Lord, I accept myself as God's perfect gift to me. If I had the choice of being anyone in the world, I would choose to be me. If I had the power to change myself, physically, emotionally, or mentally, I would not change anything. For I recognize that God does have that power and with His foreknowledge made me the way I am. He can change me if He so chooses. Failure to recognize myself, as the creation of God is to resist His will. It is in effect saying if I were God, I would change things. I accept my wife and or husband as God's perfect gift to me. If I had the power to change him or her, I wouldn't change them in anyway, and I would leave them the way they are. For God does have that power and has chosen to allow them to be who they are. All the irritations, which come about as a result of this relationship, God allowed by His permissive will. Therefore, these irritations are God's heavenly sandpaper knocking off my rough edges. When God has finished with me He will take care of these irritations.

In the same way accept your parents, children, neighbors, and employers, etc. Thank God for each of them and recognize that all the irritations that come from others are God's heavenly sandpaper for your life.

Thought Provoking Questions

1. Why should every believer accept him or herself as a perfect gift from God?

2. Why is it necessary to view the problems encountered in life as blessings or should they be?

3. Why should a believer view the things that irritate as heavenly sandpaper?

4. Why should I accept myself when my emotions and mind are in denial?

5. Is self-acceptance the same as self-love and self esteem?

6. Do most believers practice accepting the sovereignty of God?

7. What are some ways to implement the acceptance of self in daily activities?

† Warfare Prayer

Father, I have disliked my person for years. I know the Bible teaches me to accept myself. Sometimes I feel like a failure, rejected, and unloved. I confess this attitude. I confess the sin of self-centeredness and acknowledge Your love for me. I accept that You are the Potter and I am the clay, mold me and make me according to your purpose and will. I accept myself as Your creation and thank you that I am who I am. I recognize the things that irritate me You allow, and is the Holy Spirit's finger convicting me of an area of my life, which isn't under your control. I will begin to praise You for these irritations and ask You to strengthen me in the area of weakness. I will begin by thanking You for allowing irritations to come into my life. I confess that in the past I have resented these irritations. However, to resent them is in effect degrading You as God and elevating self to be God. I am fully submitting to You and have the freedom to resist the devil in Your name. I desire You to be Lord of my mind and emotions. I asked the Holy Spirit to bring to my mind past incidents that make me feel unwanted and disliked. I want to be cleansed from the power of past events.

STEPS OF ACTION

- Each day for at least ten times, stand in front of a mirror and state aloud, I am a person of worth and value. I accept myself as God has created me. If I had the power to change myself, I would not change anything, about my person. God does have that power and He chose to make me as I am. I thank God that I am, who I am.

- Once a day, think about members of the family who seem to be a source of irritation and say silently or aloud, I accept you as God created you. All of those little irritations, which drive me up the wall, are being used by God to point out my weaknesses. I count these irritations as God's heavenly sandpaper. He is using that sandpaper to knock off my rough edges.

- Each time some person, friend, family member, or neighbor becomes a source of irritation, praise God for the opportunity to praise Him in everything. Say aloud to yourself, I accept the irritation and situation as permitted by God to be a maturing factor to grow me spiritually.

18

- Remind yourself, as often as it comes to mind, that following these steps of action requires an act of faith. This means you accept yourself and others even if your emotions balk at it. It is saying to your emotions, you will not control me. I will allow God's Spirit to express Himself through me. Paul wrote, *"And do not get drunk with wine, for that is dissipation, but be filled with the Spirit."* Ephesians 5:18. The word filled means to be controlled. When a Christian declares something is true when the emotions are not concurring, it requires faith.

Chapter 2

A Principle for Controlling the Emotions

Romans 11:33-12:2

The following are a few questions, which need to be answered before a believer begins this study. Be honest and answer each question without supposing what God would have you write.

1. In your opinion, what does it mean to be a disciple of the Lord?

2. What does it mean to make Christ the Lord of one's life?

3. What does the word sacrifice mean regarding a Christian's life?

4. If you were to measure your commitment to the Lord with 10 being the highest and 1 being the lowest, where would you be? In your opinion where does the Lord expect believers to be?

5. Has there been a time in the past when you were more committed to the Lord?

Introduction

As submission to sovereignty, discussed in the first chapter, is **basic** for controlling the emotions, so **self-sacrifice is the principle** by which emotions are placed under God's control. When believers live in accord with the world's standards, rather than God's standards, this creates emotional turmoil. Believers are living contrary to their inner spiritual nature. Christians have been recreated and are indwelt with the Holy Spirit. An unbeliever can commit the same sin, committed by a believer, without emotional turmoil, since he is living in harmony with his nature. Believers have been recreated, born again. Therefore, believers must die to the urges of the flesh.

When an unbeliever commits a transgression, it is in harmony with the flesh. However, when a believer commits the same transgression it is out of harmony with the inner man and thus creates greater emotional storms. The answer to this problem is sacrificial living. *Sacrificial living is the principle of a living death.* The term sacrifice, as used in religious rituals, is foreign to Americans. In other parts of the world, this term is more commonly understood. When Americans think of sacrifice, it usually involves giving up a wanted or needed object to show selflessness. A sacrifice to the Jewish mind meant death. In order to understand the passage in Romans 12:1-2, it is essential to look at Paul's first statement. Paul said, *"I urge you therefore..."* whenever you see therefore, you should ask, what it is there for? The therefore was referring to the exhortation found in Romans 11:33-36. Paul used this passage to contrast God's sovereignty, His person, His power, and man's weakness. Therefore on the basis of 11:33-36, he gave this principle of death living as depicted in Romans 12:1-2.

> *Text*: *"Oh, the depth of the riches both of the wisdom and knowledge of God! How unsearchable are His judgments and unfathomable His ways! For who has known the mind of the Lord, or who became His counselor? Or who has first given to Him that it might be paid back to Him again? For from Him and through Him and to Him are all things. To Him be the glory forever. Amen. I urge you therefore, brethren*

> *by the mercies of God, to present your bodies a living and holy sacrifice, acceptable to God, which is your spiritual service of worship. And do not be conformed to this world, but be transformed by the renewing of your mind, that you may prove what the will of God is, that which is good and acceptable and perfect."* Romans 11:33-36-12:1-2.

The Reason for Sacrificial Living

THE MAJESTY OF GOD'S WISDOM

The passage in chapter 11 is the foundation, which encourages the believer to live a sacrificial life. The majesty of God's wisdom should be an encouragement to any believer to become a living sacrifice. This passage reveals God's wisdom and the inadequacy of man's knowledge. These thoughts could compose another exposition, so I will review them briefly. This passage shows the degree of God's wisdom and the denial of man's wisdom. Prior to exhorting believers to present their bodies a living sacrifice, Paul reminds the Roman Christians of the ultimate of God's wisdom. This passage could be applied in the prior exposition of accepting oneself. In accepting oneself it is essential to realize the wisdom of God exceeds the limit of man's knowledge and wisdom. To be willing to be a living sacrifice requires a living faith in a sovereign God. Paul lays this foundation in this passage. He wrote, *"For who has known the mind of the Lord, or who became His counselor?"* Since He is the God of all creation, the Creator of all things, who is man to question His motives or purpose. God is not indebted to man; man is indebted to God.

THE MAJESTY OF GOD'S WORK

Paul wrote, *"For from Him."* This reveals the truth that indeed all things come from God. He is sovereign over all creation. All things are under His control. This passage sets the stage for the believer's willingness to be a complete sacrifice. It elevates the Lord to the lofty position as the Creator of all things. *"And through Him"* indicates that nothing happens without His permission. This permission may be a set of operational laws that operate the world. Yet in God's wisdom He planned the universe and nothing catches Him by surprise. *"And to Him are all things. To Him be the glory forever amen."* Many believers acknowledge the sovereignty of God verbally without putting their trust in Him as Lord. To say He is Lord is one thing, to act in faith and allow Him to be Lord is another. Lordship is more than mental agreement with God. It involves commitment as expressed in Romans 12:1-2. Commitment has different meanings to Christians. This is the reason for the next study.

What Does It Mean to be Born Again?

Before a study of Romans 12:1-2, it is necessary to make certain each reader and student are believers. What does it mean to be saved? Can a person be saved without making Christ Lord of their life? Paul wrote, *"I have been crucified with Christ; and it is no longer I who live, but Christ lives in me; and the life which I now live in the flesh I live by faith in the Son of God, who loved me, and delivered Himself up for me."* Galatians 2:20. If anyone wants to be a member of God's family, they must first recognize they are a sinner. The Bible tells us in Romans 6:23 that every person who has ever been born has sinned. The penalty for our sin is eternal death or separation from God. (Read Romans 3:23 and 6:23.)

There is no way any of us can ever right the wrongs we have committed. Our situation is hopeless. But God is a loving, forgiving Creator. He does not want anyone to face this inevitable doom. On the other hand, God is so holy and pure that He cannot tolerate even a whiff of sin. Sounds impossible, doesn't it? Since humans are sinful, they cannot pay the penalty for their own sin. That would be like a pig who, lives in a mud hole being able to wash him self. Only a perfect God is able to cleanse us from sin. As unlimited Deity, He could be in heaven and on earth at the same time. So He came to earth in a human body, born as a baby, Jesus Christ. Jesus lived a perfect, sinless life, and then He died on a Roman cross to pay the penalty for our sins. Jesus took on Himself the punishment for the sins of the world, every one of them!

His death made a way for us to be forgiven of our sins and declared righteous by God. Because of Jesus, we can be pardoned and no longer face an eternal separation from God. The most difficult aspect of this pardon has to do with our will. The scripture says, *"If you confess with your mouth Jesus as Lord, and believe in your heart that God raised Him from the dead, you will be saved." Romans 10:9.*

Confession is an open declaration and commitment to Jesus as Savior and Lord. It means an absolute surrender of your will and life to Him, to *"believe in your heart."* There is a huge difference between head belief and heart belief. Imagine a famous daredevil preparing to jump twenty semi trucks with a motorcycle. He asks the crowd, "Do you believe I can jump these trucks with someone on the bike with me?" The crowd roars it approval. They believe with their heads that he can do it. Then the daredevil challenges the people. "Who will get on the bike with me?" This would require a commitment beyond what most people would be willing to commit to. Believing in your heart literally means to exchange your life for the life of Christ. Reread Galatians 2:20 and ask yourself this questions. "Is my life, literally the life of Christ?" "Have I exchanged my life for His life?" If not, before you continue exploring this exposition; make a total commitment of your life to Him.

The Requirement for Sacrificial Living - Romans 12:1

The blessing in the exhortation

*"I **urge** you therefore brethren; by the mercies of God, to present your bodies a living and holy sacrifice, acceptable to God, which is your spiritual service of worship."* The word urge reveals Paul's desire for the Roman Christians. *"Urge,"* in the Greek is *parakalio*, which means, to beseech, to encourage, and to exhort. It is one of the tenderest of expressions. It pictures a believer who in a loving spirit comes alongside another believer, while placing an arm around the other believer, lovingly pleads with that believer. It is to comfort and to bless. This is a root word from which comes the word paraklete in reference to the Holy Spirit. When Paul used "brethren," it was a very endearing term expressing love. He readily places himself as a fellow believer. His exhortation is not from

a position of authority as an apostle but as a fellow servant. Paul as a loving brother is strongly encouraging the believers in Rome to make a sacrificial commitment.

The basis for the exhortation

Paul gave the basis for the exhortation when he wrote, *"...by the mercies of God."* Note it is not mercy but mercies. This word is used nine times in chapters 9 and 11. *"Mercies"* is the outward manifestation of pity. It assumes need on behalf of the one receiving it. It is on the basis of God's mercies that Christians have the privilege of serving. The basis for a Christian's privilege of serving and being a living sacrifice is God's mercy. When Paul used mercies in this passage it probably denotes the grace of God, which reveals His love for mankind. Ministry or service to God is not an earned privilege granted because of man's importance. Man is unworthy to serve, and serve only by God's mercy and grace.

The message in sacrificial living

IT IS AN ACT OF WORSHIP

The message in sacrificial living is, *"...to **present** your bodies."* *"Present"* is an aorist imperative. Its meaning is to present, to yield, to surrender, and to place at the disposal of another. The aorist denotes a decisive act. This carries the idea of an Old Testament sacrifice. When a sacrifice was offered, the offerer would place his hands upon the head of the live animal suggesting the transference of his life to that animal. The animal became a substitute for the offerer. Paul uses the term "bodies" which indicates the whole of man. There was no room in the Jewish sacrificial system for a partial sacrifice. The demand is not to give a hand or a foot, but your all.

The principle behind the sacrificial system was obedience and loyalty to God. Sacrifice was part of worship, but without obedience it was worthless. In the Old Testament the prophet Samuel said to King Saul" *"Has the Lord as much delight in burnt offerings and sacrifices as in obeying the voice of the Lord? Behold, to obey is better than sacrifice and to heed, than the fat of rams."* 1 Samuel 15:22.

Most people would find it easier to allow others to be a living sacrifice, but the Lord demands a sacrifice of self. The Lord is not asking a believer to literally die. Rather He is asking believers to live a life of daily sacrifice. It is to become a living dead man. It is to be dead to sin, self and ungodly desires. Jesus said, *"If anyone wishes to come after Me, let him deny himself, and take up his cross, and follow Me."* Mark 8:34. To be a living sacrifice or to take up one's cross necessitates self-surrender. It is the ultimate in self-denial. As an animal became the substitute for the Old Testament saint, Jesus was the "Lamb of God that takes away the sin of the world." He became a believer's substitute. The difference is the life we live is the life of Christ. Salvation is exchanging your life for the life of Christ.

Believers living where there is little or no persecution as a result of becoming a believer are not called on by outside forces to deny the Lord or face death. When I visited an African country in 1993, I viewed a gravesite of a woman who was seven months pregnant when she was murdered. She paid the ultimate sacrifice by accepting Jesus Christ as her Lord. Because of her decision to follow the Lord, the national religion of that country stoned her, and she died four days later. Most believers will never face the prospect of death if they will not deny the Lord. However, believers should die to self by living a sacrificial life, so when the evil day comes, they will stand for the Lord.

IT IS AN ACT OF SACRIFICE

Paul describes the sacrifice as, *"... a living and holy sacrifice."* The term "sacrifice" referred to any animal sacrificed to the Lord as part of the offerings. It probably had reference to the burnt offering rather than the sin or trespass offering. A sacrifice meant death. When a sacrifice was offered, the offerer would kill the lamb by slitting its' throat. The lamb was the offerer's substitute. The offerer was vicariously cutting his own throat. When Paul wrote exhorting them to be a living sacrifice, the Jews understood this concept of projecting one's life as living dead men. Jesus became the sacrifice for mankind, it required His death. John the Baptist said, *"Behold the Lamb of God who takes away the sin of the world!"* John 1:29. Jesus became the substitute for men as the Lamb of God. As a lamb was slain as a sacrifice for men, Jesus was slain as a sacrifice for men.

"Living" is in contradiction to sacrifice. All sacrifices meant death. Thus it is a living death. Throughout Paul's writings, he stresses dying daily. He wrote in Galatians 2:20, *"I have been crucified with Christ,*

and it is no longer I, who live, but Christ lives in me and the life which I now live in the flesh I live by faith in the Son of God, who loved me, and delivered Himself up for me." Paul exhorted the Roman Christians to become living dead men. This requires dying to one's self interests and making Christ Lord in daily living. This passage has the same emphasis as Romans 6:1-14. It does not refer to literal death but death to the principle and power of sin. In this passage Paul wrote, *"Even so consider yourselves to be dead to sin, but alive to God in Christ Jesus."* Romans 6:11.

The word *"Holy"* signifies to be separated. It is used in the New Testament as separated from sin and dedicated to God. In reference to an animal, it would indicate clean, perfect and without blemish. The believer's life, including the body and soul, is to be presented to the Lord as a holy sacrifice. This means believers should be separated from the world and devoted to the Lord. Fire was used to consume a sacrifice and a believer is to be purged and refined by the fire of the Holy Spirit's convicting power. God rejected unholy sacrifices. The Lord spoke about this matter through the prophet Malachi, *"You are presenting defiled food upon My altar. But you say, 'How have we defiled Thee?' In that you say the table of the Lord is to be despised. But when you present the blind for sacrifice, is it not evil? And when you present the lame and sick, is it not evil?"* Malachi 1:7-8. Therefore, God will reject Christians as living sacrifices who continue in unholy practices. Sin must be confessed and the practice stopped.

IT IS TO BE AN ACCEPTABLE SACRIFICE

Paul indicated a sacrifice should be acceptable to God. The word *"acceptable,"* is a combination of two words, *eu* meaning well and *areston* meaning pleasing. Acceptable could be translated well pleasing. An offering could be rejected even though it was a perfect animal, if the motive of the person was wrong. This is seen in 1 Samuel 15:21-22. Saul grew tired of waiting on Samuel and took the place of the priest and offered sacrifices to God. Samuel's warning to Saul was, *"Has the Lord as much delight in burnt offerings and sacrifices as in obeying the voice of the Lord? Behold, to obey is better than sacrifice, and to heed than the fat of rams. For rebellion is as the sin of divination, and insubordination is as iniquity and idolatry."* The Psalmist wrote, *"The sacrifices of God are a broken spirit; a broken and a contrite heart, O God, Thou wilt not despise."* Psalm 51:17. To be well pleasing is to worship with a pure heart. The tendency is to compare self to other believers, rather than measuring up to the standards of God.

The word translated *"service,"* is *latreia*. This word was used to describe the ministry of the priest, in the ministry of the tabernacle or temple. It was used to describe his ministry in offering sacrifices for the worshipers. A believer is a priest of God to himself and to God. He offers up himself, to the Lord. Peter describes this concept; *"you also, as living stones, are being built up as a spiritual house for a holy priest hood, to offer up spiritual sacrifices acceptable to God through Jesus Christ."* 1 Peter 2:5. Believers are a *"holy priesthood"* and need to act like it. This describes worship in its highest expression.

The word *"spiritual"* is *logikos*, which means that which pertains to reason, or rational thinking. The King James Version uses the word *"reasonable service."* It could be translated logical service. It is no doubt a spiritual service. It is worship that derives its character by involving one's mind, reason and intellect. It is not a mechanical ritual but a rational decision. This is worship and serving in obedience not through an emotional experience. One might say, "But I don't have that fuzzy feeling about this kind of commitment." Worship is not based on feelings but obedience and submission. Feelings and the resulting emotions are the result of obedience, not the cause for obedience. As one gives his life as a living sacrifice, he is acting as a priest, making an offering to God, performing as a minister of worship.

The Method of Sacrificial Living - Romans 12:2

THE NEGATIVE COMMAND

Paul describes the method of sacrificial living, *"And do not be conformed to this world."* The word conformed, *summorphize* is a combination of *sum*, meaning with and *morphe*, meaning form. Thus, it is to make of like form with another person or thing, to render like, to form or mold after something. Conformed is a present passive imperative. As an imperative it is a command to believers not to be conformed to this world. This means the world should not be molding the believer. The word "world," *aion*, is translated age. It is a time viewed in relation to what takes place in that period of time. Here "world" relates to a period of time marked by moral and spiritual characteristics. This admonition refers to the customs and life-styles of the age.

The believer is not to mold his life around the fashions of a sinful time. This type of age is not the pattern for a believer's life. A believer who molds his/her life around the customs of the world loses spiritual vitality. The present tense use of "conformed" calls for continuous action. It is a day after day commitment or resolve not to act like the world. This command is the negative side to a positive conclusion. It is not a matter of conforming, which is so easy; it is a matter of being transformed.

THE POSITIVE COMMAND

Paul gives the alternative to conforming to the world. He commands the believer to, "*be transformed by the renewing of your mind.*" The word transformed in the Greek is *metamorpheo*, and is a combination of *meta*, with, implying change and *morpheo*, a form. *Morpheo* lays stress on the inner change. This is the same word used to describe the transfiguration of Jesus. Paul was commanding a believer to be transformed. This word is also a present passive imperative. It is a command to have an inner transformation. The present tense indicates a continuous process working toward a completion. The English word metamorphosis is a derivative of this word. It describes a larva of an insect changing into a pupa. The command is very strong, since it prohibits conforming to the world and demands a changed life. A butterfly has been transformed from an ugly worm into a beautiful insect. So it can be with Christians. However, unlike an insect, it is a gradual process of maturing.

The method of the transforming is "by the renewing of the mind." The word renewing is from the Greek word *anakainosis*. It is a combination of *ana*, meaning back or back again and *kainos*, meaning new, not recent, but different. This is a gradual restoration of the divine image in man. Man is to become more and more like God on the spiritual level. This is called sanctification. The renewing of the mind is shaking off the world's way of thinking and acting and allowing the Spirit of God to control the thought process. Ultimately the inward behavior of a believer should determine the outward renewal process. The word mind in the Greek is *nous*. This word involves the whole gamut of one's thoughts, actions and emotions. It controls negative thinking, depression, rejection, etc. The renewal of the mind is accomplished by an active effort of the believer to be under control of the Holy Spirit and not under the influence of the world. The next few pages will enlarge on this practical process. The essence of this study is the renewal of the mind or being transformed. We are to be like God since He lives in us.

The Results of Sacrificial Living

PROVING THE WILL OF GOD

Paul indicates a believer does have something to prove. He wrote, *"...that you may prove what the will of God is, that which is good and acceptable and perfect."* The word "prove" is the Greek word *dokimazo*, which means to prove by testing or to accept as approved after testing. Prove is an infinitive and expresses purpose or result. Believers thus prove the principle of God in man. They also prove God's purpose is right and correct. Living an undisciplined, uncontrolled life proves to the world God's purposes and will are not the guiding principles for one's life. A major reason more people do not respect and follow God is the careless life of believers. This scripture indicates the believer is to be God's light to the world. This proof is both personal and public. Trials in life provide the believer an opportunity to prove to self and others God's faithfulness.

APPROVING THE WILL OF GOD

Since *prove* means to test, the testing is for the purpose of approving and finding the thing tested meets the specification laid down. This finds the will of God as, that, which is *"good,"* that which is *"acceptable"* or well pleasing, and that which is *"perfect."* Perfect does not mean without sin, but mature. When believers are to be perfect, they are to be mature. Acceptance of these commands and the resulting obedience is revealing a believer's approval of God's will. A failure to become a living sacrifice is showing a disapproval of God's will. How can a believer approve of something he rejects? Can the will of God be perfect? Can it also be pleasing? If the answer is yes and it should be, then why not do it? However this requires a total sacrifice of self. It also requires the daily determination of renewing the mind. It is the practice of faith daily. Faith requires one to believe, regarding God's will without seeing the finished results. Faith is trusting in God to provide for every need, by ceasing to be in charge of your life.

Real Life Illustration

As a young man I was taught to be a committed believer, and one should confess sins. I would confess sins in a block by saying, "Father, forgive me for all my sins." This did not alleviate the conviction or the guilt of sin. In the early seventies I learned a truth, sins need to be confessed individually not collectively. As a result of reading a sin sheet, I spent time writing down my sins and confessing them. After confession the sheet was destroyed. The next step was to accept God's forgiveness. This was an act of faith. It was necessary to remind the mind and emotions that God had forgiven and the mind and emotions must accept His forgiveness. Needless to say the evil one reminded the mind of previous sins and attempted to place me on a guilt trip. The confession of sin is agreeing with God about the sin or sins. Repenting is dying to self and agreeing to live like Jesus.

Verbal Commitment to the Lord

Repeat the following to another person or to the Lord, I am reminded of the last chapter's exhortation to accept others and myself. I again thank God for all of the irritations that have come into my life this week. I will again express my acceptance of self. I am reminded that Paul wrote, *"For from Him and through Him and to Him are all things. To Him be the glory forever. Amen."* This passage states that all things are from Him. I thank Him for all things. Failure to accept myself is to reject being a living sacrifice. I thank God that I can be a living dead person. I ask the Lord to remind me of any unconfessed sins and I will willingly confess them and not practice them again. I am willing to commit my life to Him. My desire is to allow my mind to be renewed, that I may prove through my life *"what the will of God is, that which is good and acceptable and perfect.*

Thought Provoking Questions

1. In your opinion what does the Bible mean by a living sacrifice?

2. If God wants us to be a living sacrifice, being a sinner, how can we be holy?

3. What makes a believer's life acceptable to God?

4. What do believers have to avoid so they will not conform to this world?

5. In your opinion how can a believer renew the mind?

6. How can believers prove the will of God?

7. What are some practical ways to implement this passage in everyday living?

† Warfare Prayer

Father, I willfully commit my life to you. I accept for myself Galatians 2:20. *"I have been crucified with Christ; and it is no longer I who live, but Christ lives in me; and the life which I now live in the flesh I live by faith in the Son of God, who loved me, and delivered Himself up for me."* I ask you to reveal to me any area of my life in which I do not place you first. I ask that the Holy Spirit would convict me each time I exercise control over my life. I understand presenting my life as a living sacrifice makes me a living dead person. I choose to die to sin and live out the life of Christ. I ask the Holy Spirit to convict me when I choose to be conformed to this world. I choose to be transformed. I will allow the Holy Spirit to begin the process of renewing my mind and emotions, bringing them into conformity with Your will. I ask You to defuse anything occurring in the past, which has power to limit my Christian walk.

STEPS OF ACTION

- When you awaken each morning, make it a point to say aloud, I do not live; I gave this life and body to the Lord. It is not mine; I was bought with a price. I am willing to become a living sacrifice.

- Make a decision to live a holy life, one that will be pleasing to the Lord. This will require you to react to pressures in the same manner as Jesus. You might say, "God is in control of my life and anything which happens to me today, does not happen to me, but to the Lord who lives in me."

- Decide each and every day that your life will not conform to the world's standards. State aloud, I have decided to please God not man. Outside influences will not dictate how I live.

- Answer the following questions periodically; have I neglected to be pleasing to God in all things? Have I complained against Him in any way? Am I willing to obey God fully? Do I have any reservations as to anything that might be His will? Have I disobeyed any direct leading from Him? Does anything mean more to me than living for and pleasing God?

- As an added thought you could pray daily, Father I am totally committed to you. I ask the Holy Spirit to prick my conscience when I assume control of my life or start conceding to the world's standards.

Chapter 3

✆

The Principle of Renewing the Mind
Colossians 3:1-3; Romans 12:1-2; Ephesians 4:22-23

The following are a few questions, which need to be answered before a believer begins this study. Be honest and answer each question without supposing what God would have you write.

1. Do you think it is possible to renew the mind?

2. Can a believer renew the mind without the power of the Holy Spirit?

3. Is renewing the mind a principle called positive thinking?

4. Is there anything arising out of the mind which tends to control your actions?

5. If you could change any emotion, which one would it be?

Introduction

In Chapter 12:2, Paul called for the renewing the mind. This chapter begins the quest of learning this principle of renewing the mind. This principle of renewing the mind is not described in detail in the Bible, but is derived from a variety of verses. The importance of controlling your thinking is revealed in Proverbs 23:7, *"For as he thinks within himself so is he."* Paul writes in I Corinthians 14:20, *"Brethren, do not be children in your thinking, yet in evil be babes, but in your thinking be mature."*

The old nature, the flesh, desires that a believer's thoughts be under its power. In Isaiah 55:8-9, the Lord states through the prophet Isaiah, *"For my thoughts are not your thoughts."*

The challenges of Paul's writings indicate a renewal of one's thinking, which is in reality the process of sanctification. The study in Romans 12:2, indicated believers are to be *"... transformed by the renewing of the mind."* In this passage in Colossians, Paul commands a believer to *"Set your mind on things above."* In Ephesians 4:22-23, Paul states, *"That in reference to your former manner of life, you lay aside the old self, which is being corrupted in accordance with the lusts of deceit and that you be renewed in the spirit of your mind."* In Philippians 4:8, Paul lists the values in good thinking, *"...whatever is honorable, whatever is right, whatever is pure, whatever is lovely, whatever is of good repute, if there is any excellence and if there is anything worthy of praise, let your mind dwell on these things."*

> **Text**: *If then you have been raised up with Christ, keep seeking the things above, where Christ is, seated at the right hand of God. Set your mind on the things above, not on the things that are on earth. For you have died and your life is hidden with Christ in God. Colossians 3:1-3.*

THE FACTORS IN RENEWING THE MIND

The condition of faith - Col. 3:1a

Paul started this principle by writing *"If then..."* As used here if is a condition as fulfilled. It can be translated since. It could read, "Since you have been raised up with Christ." Of course they had been raised up, or received salvation. *"If"*, introduces a conditional sentence, which assumes the reality of a complete action. In the English language if means maybe or perhaps. This should not be assumed to mean perhaps believers have been raised up. Paul wrote in the preceding chapter, *"... having been buried with Him in baptism, in which you were also raised up with Him through faith in the working of God, who raised Him from the dead."* Colossians 2:12. Being raised up speaks of the new birth as well as a future resurrection.

THE MEANING OF THE RESURRECTION

The word *"raised up"* is *sunegeiro* and means to be co-raised. It is composed of two Greek words *sun*, "with" and *egeiro*, "to raise up". It is an aorist passive indicating a completed act in past time. This was accomplished for the believer in the resurrection of Christ. If in His death, all who believe died and they did, then certainly in His resurrection all are made alive and they are. Paul describes this in 2 Corinthians 5:17, *"Therefore if any man be in Christ, he is a new creature; the old things passed away; behold new things have come."* This is more than a future resurrection; it is a spiritual resurrection and a reality that occurs as a result of the new birth. Paul describes the resurrected life in Romans 6:4ff, *"Therefore we have been buried with Him through baptism into death, in order that as Christ was raised from the dead through the glory of the Father, so we too might walk in newness of life."* Through regeneration a believer is resurrected from the sin nature and will be resurrected from the body after death.

THE METHOD OF RESURRECTION

It is not to be raised up with any hope but to be *raised up with Christ*. To be raised up with Christ describes the certainty of a spiritual transformation and the cause of that transformation. This transformation is on the level of the spirit. Naturally at the time of the born-again experience the soul and body are still housed in their earthly shell. However, the spirit of a person is miraculously changed and it boggles the mind to think that an earthly creature can be *in Christ*. Paul wrote, *"...and raised us up with Him, and seated us with Him in the heavenly places, in Christ Jesus..."* Ephesians 2:6. It is also an assurance of a future resurrection. Paul wrote in 1 Corinthians 14:42, *"So also is the resurrection of the dead. It is sown a perishable body, it is raised and imperishable body."* The fact of the resurrection of Jesus is the assurance of a believer's present and future resurrection. This is why Paul could indicate that believers were in *"...heavenly places in Christ Jesus."* When Jesus was raised, God through His marvelous plan co-raised all believers. Naturally this becomes a reality for each individual when they receive the Lord. It will also become reality after death and believers are raised to live eternally with God.

The command to follow

"Keep seeking" in the Greek is *zeteo*, and means to seek for or to strive after. *"Seeking"* is a present imperative, which is a command with continuous action. This is a strong command and not something done at your leisure. One must immediately wonder what God wants a believer to seek. Paul was stressing to have the right attitude in your daily walk. The attitude should be "I will seek the mind of God daily and not just float through life." It would be easy if a believer could say presto and the mind and emotions was brought under control. God does not do the transforming of the mind and controlling the emotions, without man's help. It is accomplished when a believer puts forth effort over a period of time desiring to grow in spiritual maturity with God's help. Because "keep seeking," is in the present tense, Paul calls for a life-style of seeking the mind of God.

Peter described it in I Peter 1:13, *"Therefore gird up your minds for action, keep sober in spirit, fix your hope completely on the grace to be brought to you at the revelation of Jesus Christ."* This is not a Sunday commitment but a daily seeking of God. It is more than having a quiet time; it is a full time task of fixing your mind on the things above. It is becoming heavenly minded. It is developing the habit of seeking the mind of God in the face of life's problems. Without the strength of the Lord it is not easy mentally and emotionally to roll with the punches of life. This command reminds believers to take their eyes off the problems of life and focus them on God. A good habit to develop is to ask the Lord to give order to each day. Tell Him, "Whatever happens today is in accord with Your permissive will and does not catch You by surprise. I know what ever happens is an opportunity to exercise faith. Faith believes You will cause things to work for good. I dedicate myself to seek above things for the day and not get caught up in today's troubles."

The center of one's focus

Paul makes the statement *"The things above, where Christ is,"* in a different way in Philippians 4:8. *"Finally brethren, whatever is true, whatever is honorable, whatever is right, whatever is pure, whatever is lovely, whatever is of good repute, if there is any excellence and if anything worthy of praise, let your mind dwell on these things."* When living in the world, it is difficult to keep your mind off of life's problems and on the Lord. There is a song, which reminds believers to, "Turn your eyes upon Jesus, look full into His wonderful face, and the things of earth will grow strangely dim in the light of His glory and grace." When the children of Israel marched around Jericho, the ark led the way. Since the ark represented the presence of God, this communicated the idea of keeping their eyes focused on the Lord and not on the walls. Why look at the impossible, when you can look on Him who makes possible the impossible.

Another hymn states, "This world is not my home, I'm just passing through." This is the crux of this passage. A believer should view each problem as it relates to God and eternity. Most problems viewed from eternity's point of view are nothing. It would amaze most Christians if they wrote down the problems creating anxiety and fear, and look at them a month later. They would find most of the problems were not problems, but opportunities for walking in faith, growing spiritually and maturing emotionally.

The next portion of a verse used by Paul is, *"Seated at the right hand of God."* The right hand of a person of authority is a position of honor. It is also a position of power. The mother of James and John made this request: *"Command that in Your kingdom these two sons of mine may sit, one on Your right and one on Your left."* Matthew 20:21. Jesus response to James and John was, *"You do not know what you are asking for, are you able to drink the cup that I am about to drink?"* In other words you are not able to take My place beside the Father. <u>For Christ to be seated at the right hand of the Father reveals glory, power, position and the ability to make intercession for the saints</u>. This should reassure believers that Jesus knows what is happening in each individual's life. It communicates that everything is under His control. He is the victor over death and hell and makes intercession for His saints.

The contrast with the flesh

Paul wrote, *"Set your mind."* The Greek word for mind is *phroneo*. It is used as a present imperative and means to think or be minded in a certain way. To renew the mind indicates a previous mindset. This mindset indicates a fleshly, negative, sinful way of thinking and acting. All men and women are born with a worldly mind. Emotions that are often described as the desires of the flesh are the result of a thought process. These emotions become controlling as they develop into habits. Paul explained the conflict with the Spirit and the flesh in Galatians 5:16-17, *"But I say walk by the Spirit and you will not carry out the desire of the flesh, for the flesh sets its desire against the Spirit and the Spirit against the flesh, for these are in opposition to one another,*

41

so that you may not do the things that you please." The flesh has the ability to control your thinking. A born again experience does not erase the accumulation of past thoughts nor eliminate the habitual ways of reacting to emotional stimuli.

The new birth gives the believer the inward power to overcome these strong desires, but it does not eliminate them. If the new birth eliminated these ungodly desires there would not be a need to renew the mind. However, believers were commanded to be transformed through the renewing of the mind. Paul also wrote in Ephesians 5:25, *"if we live by the Spirit, let us also walk by the Spirit."* Found in the second chapter of this book, Paul stated the principle for living by the Spirit, a death life. *"I urge you therefore, brethren by the mercies of God, to present your bodies a living and holy sacrifice, acceptable to God, which is your spiritual service of worship. And do not be conformed to this world, but be transformed by the renewing of your mind, that you may prove what the will of God is, that which is good and acceptable and perfect."* Romans 12:1-2.

Also the emphasis is on renewing the mind. This is accomplished by allowing the power of God to change the natural bent of a carnal mind. Paul wrote to the Ephesians, *"But I say, walk by the Spirit, and you will not carry out the desire of the flesh."* Ephesians 5:16. Paul commanded that believers *"be filled with the Holy Spirit."* Ephesians 5:18. Filled is a present imperative. It is a command with the continuing results of being filled. If a glass is filled with orange juice and someone bumps the hand, what will spill from the glass? Would it be water or orange juice? When life's problems shake a believer's life what spills forth is what he is filled with. If anger spills forth he is filled with anger. If praise comes forth he is filled with praise. Renewing the mind is allowing the indwelling Spirit to change what emerges, when a believer's life gets turned upside down. This same challenge is seen in Romans 8:5, *"For those who are according to the flesh set their minds on the things of the flesh, but those who are according to the Spirit the things of the Spirit."*

Real Life Illustration

The following shows the truth of the principle of renewing the mind. The young man's name is not used but it is a true story. I once counseled a nineteen-year-old Christian named David. He was struggling with severe emotional problems, which had a death-grip on his life. In fact, he had attempted suicide on several occasions. He did not like himself and wished he was someone else. He was rebelling against authority and using drugs. In our first session, he admitted his life was out of control and ruled by sin not by God. He did have a desire to walk with God. We worked through some material and which showed him how to detail his sins and begin destroying the strongholds in his life. From that day forward his life changed. God begin, through David's commitment, to renew the mind and control the emotions. He has now finished graduate school in preparation for the ministry.

THE PRACTICE OF FAITH

The practice of faith is essential for victory over the flesh. The mind and emotions can be controlled by faith. What one believes, can determine what one thinks. Faith as defined in Hebrews is, *"Now faith is the assurance of things hoped for, the conviction of things not seen."* Hebrews 11:1. If faith is assurance, it indicates that it is in hand. However, the writer indicates it is hoped for. In addition the writer stated the conviction or as it is in the KJV evidence of things not seen. How is it possible from the human perspective that evidence cannot be seen? A simple definition is, faith believes you have something that you don't have in order that you might receive it. Faith is acting as if it happens before it happens in order that it might happen. Faith is accepting the word of God, when the mind dictates other thoughts that go contrary to the word. In practice believers are to believe the mind is being renewed while rejecting negative and sinful thoughts.

Faith assumes the thoughts and emotions are defeated and having no power to control the mind, when it appears they do have that power. When a thought contrary to God's character enters the mind, it must be rejected. It does not matter how strong the thought, if believers are born again, they have the power to resist. This power comes through the indwelling presence of the Holy Spirit.

THE PRINCIPLE ILLUSTRATED

Think about two pit bulls in a death struggle in the middle of the road with a large truck about to run over them. A woman is screaming. How piercing the scream. In your mind can you identify with the owner of one of the dogs? You feel her pain. Now put the scene out of your mind. Often a scene like this is hard to forget, even when it is made up. The best way to forget this picture is to visualize a different scene. Visualize a man with an Irish setter in the golden grain fields of Kansas hunting pheasants. The setter comes to point. The beautiful pheasant erupts from the grass with a flutter of wings; the man swings his gun to the shoulder. You could almost scream, "Don't kill that lovely bird." Are you thinking about the dogs who are about to be run over, or the hunter, dog and pheasant? So it is in life, believers must deliberately by faith, set their minds on higher things. This will require a deliberate rejection of worldly thinking, and a determination to think on heavenly things. It also requires a constant reliance upon the Holy Spirit. When some thought grips the conscious mind, it may take repeated attempts to dislodge it. You may need to consciously think on some other matter a dozen times until you have victory over a troubling thought. If it continues, pray and ask the Holy Spirits help in putting it to flight.

Jesus revealed the source for all man's thoughts. Thoughts come from within. As the inner man is changed, there is a need to bring the fleshly mind under subjection to the inner man. He said, *"For from within, out of the heart of men, proceed the evil thoughts, fornications, thefts, murders, adultery, deeds of coveting and wickedness, as well as deceit, sensuality, envy, slander, pride and foolishness. All these evil things proceed from within and defile the man."* Mark 7:21. Everyone is born with a wicked nature and the flesh reproduces wickedness. The Spirit in man is holy and will reproduce holiness if He is allowed to work. Peter is an example of human thinking. Jesus addressed this problem as recorded by Matthew, *"From that time Jesus Christ began to show His disciples that He must go to Jerusalem, and suffer many things from the elders and chief priests and scribes, and be killed, and be raised up on the third day."* Matthew 16:21. *"Peter responded, let it not be so Lord."* Jesus responded to the motives controlling Peter's thinking, *"But He turned and said to Peter,'Get behind Me, Satan! You are a stumbling block to me for you are not setting your mind on God's interests, but man's."* Matthew 16:23. From man's way of thinking did Peter express love and compassion? Often thinking like Peter reveals sometimes good things can be used for evil. Believers need to set aside earthly ways of thinking and look at things from God's perspective.

THE FOUNDATION FOR RENEWING THE MIND

The provision of salvation

In Colossians 3:3 *"Have died"* is *apothnesko,* and means to die off or out, to separate the soul from the body or to die and be in separation from God. Believers have already died with Christ to the penalty of the law. "Died" is an aorist indicating a completed act. As previously shown Paul indicated in Romans 12:1, a believer is to be a living sacrifice. Paul wrote in Galatians 2:20, *"I am co-crucified with Christ..."* To be crucified is to die. Needless to say this death was not physical. It was dying to the power of sin. Paul in writing to the church of Rome wrote, *"Knowing this, that our old self was crucified with Him, that our body of sin might be done away with, that we should no longer be slaves to sin, for He who has died is freed from sin ... even so consider yourselves to be dead to sin but alive to God in Christ Jesus."* Romans 6:6-7,11. Paul stated in Galatians 5:24, *"Now those who belong to Christ Jesus have crucified the flesh with its passion and desires."*

This means the flesh does not have the power over a Christian unless it is giving permission by the believer. This permission will not come from the spirit of a believer. It can only occur when a believer does not allow the Holy Spirit to control. When this happens it means the believer is controlled by the flesh not the Spirit. Therefore, the believer is not accepting his death to the power of sin. In the above cited verses Paul stated, *"even so consider yourselves dead to sin." Consider* can be translated *to reckon.* This is accomplished through the thought process and trusting God to empower the believer in dying to self. A Christian believes the power of sin does not have the power to enslave. A believer sins because they choose to sin, not because it is mandatory or they can't help themselves. In a church where I pastored, a deacon with a hot temper said, "I know I have a bad temper, but that is just the way I am. I can't help myself and other people are going to have to accept me the way I am." An old saying is, "this is hogwash." This type of thinking negates the power and authority of God. It also nullifies the work of grace through the cross. All Christians have the freedom to live a victorious life as a result of the life, death and resurrection of Jesus Christ.

45

The position of salvation

The flipside of being dead to sin is to be alive to God. Paul stated in Galatians 5:25, *"If we live by the Spirit, let us also walk by the Spirit."* A believer does live by the Spirit, thus he can walk by the Spirit. Paul wrote, *"Therefore, if any man is in Christ, he is a new creature; the old things passed away, behold, new things have come."* 2 Corinthians 5:17. The only thing keeping a believer from overcoming the flesh is the desire to overcome. The Holy Spirit is the strength of Christians and enables them in becoming an over comer. Any believer who states, "This emotional hang-up has such a grip on me that I can't control my life," is saying the hang-up is too big a problem for God. The truth is the believer is not filled with the Holy Spirit, since all things are possible with God.

Paul uses the word hidden. *"Hidden"* in the Greek is *krupto*, and means to cover, conceal, or keep secret. To the world this is a mystery, to believers an open secret. A believer's life is hidden in Christ. Even believers do not easily understand this mystery. The world will never understand these types of spiritual matters. Only those who are spiritual can understand spiritual truths. *Hidden* is in the perfect tense, indicating continuous action, forever hidden. The life that is hidden has to be in the realm of the spiritual. Jesus said, *"...they are not of the world as I am not of the world. I do not ask Thee to take them out of the world, but to keep them from the evil one."* John 17:14-15. The world cannot understand the inner strength of believers. Most Christians are aware that life's problems are faced in the strength of God, and not in their own strength. The world views a belief in God as a weakness. Christians should consider it as strength and security. It is man's pride which makes him want to function without God's help. Indeed what is wrong with having God as a friend and savior?

The phrase *"With Christ in God"* is illustrated in John's gospel by Jesus, *"And I give eternal life to them, and they shall never perish and no one shall snatch them out of my hand. My Father, who has given them to Me, is greater than all; and no one is able to snatch them out of the Father's hand."* John 10:28-29. Being in the hand of the Lord, as I understand it, means under His control. The life of a believer is secure in the Lord. It is not a matter of one keeping oneself. It is a matter of being placed spiritually into Christ. Regarding this mystery Paul wrote, *"... the mystery which has been hidden from the past ages and generations; but has now been manifested to His saints, to whom God willed to make known what is the riches of the glory of this mystery among the Gentiles, which is Christ in you, the hope of glory."* Colossians 1:26-27. So not only is a believer in Christ, Christ is in the believer.

The control of your mind, thoughts and the resulting emotions is not only possible, but is commanded. It is imperative for the believer to live a Christ life. Every emotion is triggered by a thought. These thoughts result in actions and attitudes. By renewing the mind, you can bring your mind and emotions under control. A believer may fail at times in living a life in which the mind is renewed daily. These temporary lapses do not constitute failure. Paul said believers are *"...with Christ in God."* This promise should encourage and enable a believer in the pursuit of controlling the mind. As was mention in the introduction of the book, a basic passage for renewing the mind is found in 2 Corinthians 10:3-5. This passage indicates the Holy Spirit can bring into the mind traumatic experiences or events occurring in the past. Many of these traumas still affect the thinking process and emotional stability. They need to be reviewed and the power behind them eliminated. This is done by asking the Holy Spirit to bring into your mind anything occurring in the past, which creates an emotional reaction such as anger, fear, resentment, tears, etc. Write down what the Holy Spirit reveals and ask the Lord to cleanse you from any sin and power, which affect your walk with the Lord. This may require forgiving someone who has hurt you or caused your emotional grief.

Verbal Commitment to the Lord

Repeat the following to another person or to the Lord, I do believe I have the ability through the power of the Holy Spirit to control my mind. Satan and his demonic spirits delight in believers yielding to the flesh. I choose to set my mind on heavenly things, rather than earthly things. When ungodly or fleshly thoughts enter my thoughts I will deliberately think on other things. According to God's word I am dead to the power of sin. I do not have to sin. When I sin, it is because I have chosen to let the flesh control me. I will ask God to bring to my attention the times each day in which I allow my thoughts to dwell on things that displease the Lord. My prayer is to grow in the Lord. I recognize that controlling my mind helps in controlling my emotions. It helps thwart Satan's fiery darts.

47

Thought Provoking Questions

1. In your opinion what does it mean to renew the mind?

2. Can a believer grow spiritually if they don't renew the mind? If not, why not?

3. Since the mind is not renewed when one is saved, why does the Lord leave the renewing to each individual?

4. How long does it take to renew the mind?

5. Is a believer a composite of what is thought?

6. Why is it so difficult to set your mind on things above?

7. What process can you implement in your daily life to control the mental process?

8. Do emotions drive the mind or does the mind drive the emotions?

---

† Warfare Prayer

Father, I ask you to begin the process of renewing my mind. I am willing to do my part by limiting what enters the mind and what it dwells upon. I know that garbage in is garbage out. I will deliberately focus my mind on higher things. I recommit myself to the practice of setting my mind on things above and not on earthly matters. Any area of my life, which hinders this process, I ask that the Holy Spirit bring me into awareness through conviction. Father I know things are hidden in my subconscious mind, which affects the thinking process. I ask you to set me free from the power attached to these events. If any of these past reflections involve sin, I will confess it. Any emotion and every emotion that hinders this process of growing into maturity I yield to you. Show me the way to bring every aspect of my life under your control. I confess failure to control my thoughts is allowing the flesh to control my life. I choose to be filled (that is controlled) with or by the Holy Spirit.

STEPS OF ACTION

• Make a checklist of your reading material and television viewing. Clean up the things you are putting into your mind. Remember, "Garbage in, garbage out." In making this list ask yourself the following questions, Do I listen to unedifying radio and TV programs? Do I read trashy and ungodly magazines? Do I listen to dirty or smutty jokes? Do I indulge in entertainment that is unclean?

• Begin a quiet time, a time for daily devotions. A time with the Lord strengthens your ability to resist the devil in the evil day. Run your negative thoughts by Philippians 4:8. If they do not measure up to this passage, reject them.

• Learn to listen more than you speak. If you get into trouble because of what you say, memorize James 3:1-12.

• List and analyze your perceptions, prejudices and expectations. Ask yourself, do I have a habitual problem of wrong thinking which I need to correct? If so, it is a stronghold and you may need help in destroying the stronghold.

Chapter 4

                                         ❧

Depression, Emotional Self-Centeredness

1 Kings 19:1-18

The following are a few questions, which need to be answered before a believer begins this study. Be honest and answer each question without supposing what God would have you write.

1. Is depression a way of life, and there is little a person can do about it?

2. Have you ever been depressed over nothing?

3. When you get depressed, how do you get through it?

4. Is depression a sin? Are there degrees of depression? If there are degrees of depression, at what point does depression become sin?

5. Did Jesus ever get depressed?

Introduction

The word depression is not found in the Bible. Some synonyms are gloom, soul cast down, fallen countenance, despair, distress, heaviness of heart, etc. However, the Bible is filled with examples of depression. Cain was depressed because God rejected his offering. The Lord told him, *"If you do well, will not your countenance be lifted up?"* Genesis 4:7. This is one example of a person being depressed. Elijah is another example. Elijah's depth of depression is seen in I Kings 19:4, *"But he himself went a day's journey into the wilderness, and came and sat down under a juniper tree and he requested for himself that he might die, and said, 'It is enough, now O Lord, take my life, for I am not better than my fathers.'"* Ahab was depressed because he did not get what he wanted, Naboth's vineyard. Jezebel asked Ahab in I Kings 21:5, *"How is it that your spirit is so sullen that you are not eating food'?"*

Job is seen wallowing in self-pity. As recorded in chapter 3:11, Job states, *"Why did I not die at birth, come forth from the womb and expire?"* In the New Testament, Jesus in the garden of Gethsemane revealed an emotion verging on depression if not depression. Mark wrote, *"...began to be very distressed and troubled and He said to them, 'my soul is deeply grieved to the point of death...'"* Mark 14:33-34. The word *"distressed,"* *adamoneo* means to be troubled or much distressed. Jesus had a degree of depression brought about by His thoughts of separation from the Father, of becoming the sin bearer, a separation from the disciples and knowledge of their inability to stand the test of discipleship. **Not all depression is sin**. Depression's length and depth, its cause and circumstances, the reaction and the result determine its sinfulness. Depression can also be the result of a chemical imbalance in one's system.

> ***Text:*** *"'Now Ahab told Jezebel all that Elijah had done, and how he had killed all the prophets with the sword. Then Jezebel sent a messenger to Elijah, saying, "So may the gods do to me and even more, if I do not make your life as the life of one of them by tomorrow about this time.' And he was afraid and arose and ran for his life and came to Beersheba, which belongs to Judah, and left his servant there. But he himself went a day's journey into the wilderness, and came and sat down under a juniper tree; and he requested for himself that he might die, and said, 'It is enough; now O Lord, take my life, for I am not better than my fathers.' And he lay down and slept under a juniper tree; and behold, there was an angel touching him, and he said to him, 'Arise, eat.' Then he looked and behold, there was at his head a bread cake baked on hot stones, and a jar of water. So he ate and drank and lay down again.*

And the angel of the Lord came again a second time and touched him and said, 'Arise, eat, because the journey is too great for you.' So he arose and ate and drank, and went in the strength of that food forty days and forty nights to Horeb, the mountain of God. Then he came there to a cave, and lodged there; and behold, the word of the Lord came to him, and He said to him, 'What are you doing here Elijah?' And he said, 'I have been very zealous for the Lord, the God of hosts, for the sons of Israel have forsaken Thy covenant, torn down Thine altars and killed Thy prophets with the sword. And I alone am left; and they seek my life, to take it away.' So He said, 'Go forth, and stand on the mountain before the Lord.' And behold, the Lord was passing by! And a great and strong wind was rending the mountains and breaking in pieces the rocks before the Lord; but the Lord was not in the wind. And after the wind an earthquake, but the Lord was not in the earthquake and after the earthquake, a fire, but the Lord was not in the fire; and after the fire a sound of a gentle blowing. And it came about when Elijah heard it, that he wrapped his face in his mantle, and went out and stood in the entrance of the cave And behold, a voice came to him and said, 'What are you doing here Elijah?'" Then he said, 'I have been very zealous for the Lord, the God of hosts; for the sons of Israel have forsaken Thy covenant, torn down Thine altars and killed Thy prophets with the sword. And I alone am left; and they seek my life, to take it away. " And the Lord said to him, 'Go, return on your way to the wilderness of Damascus, and when you have arrived, you shall anoint Hazael king over Aram; and Jehu the son of Nimshi you shall anoint king over Israel; and Elisha the son of Shaphat of Abel-meholah you shall anoint as prophet in your place.'" 1 Kings 19:1-18

An Examination of Depression

THE DESCRIPTION OF DEPRESSION

Depression is an emotional reaction to unresolved life stresses, rooted in self-pity. Depression is the failure to have inner peace and joy. It replaces inner peace with discontentment, self-pity and unhappiness. It is a result of despair and doubt, destroying faith and hope. It is the outgrowth of negative thinking about life. It begins with the thought process. The Bible does not have a word for depression. But the Bible does describe the symptoms of depression.

Depression can be described best using H. Norman Wright's ten descriptions found in his book entitled <u>Now I Know Why I Am Depressed</u>. A depressed person experiences a general feeling of hopelessness, despair, sadness, apathy and gloom. When a person is depressed, he loses perspective. The depressed person experiences changes in physical activities. There is a general loss of self-esteem. Self-confidence is at an all time low. The depressed person withdraws from other people. There is a desire to escape from problems and even life itself. A depressed person is oversensitive to what other people say and do. The person has difficulty in handling most of his feelings, especially anger. Guilt is another characteristic of depression. Often, depression leads to a state of depending upon other people.

THE DEGREES OF DEPRESSION

Discouragement

The first step toward depression is discouragement. Discouragement is to deprive of courage, of hope or confidence, to dishearten. It is the natural enemy of faith. At this stage, it is not sin unless it is allowed to exist, dominate, control and root into prolonged depression. This is primary an attitude which exists in all of mankind. Discouragement is a normal emotional reaction when one's expectations do not materialize. It also may come as a result of feeling rejected. Discouragement originates from the level of the soul, not the spirit of a believer. Seeing things spiritually from God's perspective will alleviate discouragement.

Despondency

The second level leading to deep depression is despondency. Despondency is a loss of hope, courage and direction. It reveals a lack of desire. Physical exercise is avoided, and social encounters are a threat. Despondency turns inwardly toward self-pity. This emotional attitude creates a lethargic state. One is fully satisfied to be inactive. A depressed person is often tired without any reason. This emotional state drains or saps his energy. There is generally a feeling of "What is the use?" This kind of thought often runs through the mind, "Every time I try to get on my feet it seems something keeps knocking me down." Despondent Christians don't want to pray, because it won't do any good. As will be noted later this is a threat to a walk of faith and the opposite of having joy.

Despair

Depression is seen in its ugly and final form as despair. Despair is expressed as an attitude of total failure. There seems to be no hope. Despair as well as despondency reveals a lack of trust in God. There is a deficiency of joy or peace. One can even doubt his salvation, and cannot imagine God loves him. Prolonged depression usually brings despair. In this state many believers and others have contemplated ending their lives. Despair can cause all types of self-destructive thoughts. In a marriage it often leads to divorce. Deep despair is displaying unbelief in God. Despair says in effect, "I can't trust God to handle my problems and I can't solve them. There is no solution so why should I try any more." Needless to say, this is effective warfare brought about by the forces of wickedness with the believers cooperation. Satan's purpose is to destroy a believer's walk with God.

An Example of Depression

For three and one half years, Elijah had anticipated what God would to do to Israel, Ahab and Jezebel. Elijah had spent six months with a raven feeding him, three years with a widow. Her flour and oil never ceased, and a son was restored to life. He had prayed, and for three years there was no rain or dew. After waiting for months, God's timing for a confrontation with the prophets of Baal had arrived. On Mount Carmel after the prophets of Baal had prayed all day Elijah prayed a short prayer. Fire fell from heaven and consumed the sacrifice and even lapped up the water, which was poured over the offering and altar. As a result the 450 prophets of Baal and 400 prophets of Asherah were slain. It appeared that God was about to do a mighty thing in Israel. Then Elijah prayed seven times until God revealed it would rain.

After this miracle he ran seventeen miles, with the aid of God's Spirit, beating Ahab to Jezreel. Remember Ahab was in a chariot. He was physically and emotionally drained. Elijah apparently anticipated God's destruction of Jezebel. He was excited to see the power of God destroy the unbelievers. Instead Jezebel, after hearing the report about Elijah, threatened his life. When God did not act according to his expectations, he fled with his servant. He went ninety miles south to Beersheba, and leaving his servant, went another ten to twelve miles into the wilderness. The Bible reveals his state of depression. Notice how many of Wright's ten statements on depression fit Elijah's life.

A COMPARISON OF ELIJAH'S DEPRESSION

1. He felt hopeless despair when God failed to live up to his expectations. He must have anticipated the people revolting against Jezebel, or perhaps that God would provide some miracle, so the people would turn back to God. God had disappointed him, so he didn't wait, but ran for his life. "But he himself went a day's journey into the wilderness..." I Kings 19:4.

2. He felt fear, anxiety about his life. Elijah as a prophet stood forth defying the king and the eight hundred and fifty false prophets and then ran for his life because of Jezebel's threat. If this had happened five years later after the experience on Mt. Carmel, it would be easier understood. However, it happened on the same day. He went from hero to coward in hours not days. The question is why? Fear was a primary motivating factor making Elijah act contrary to God's standard for a prophet.

3. He lost his perspective. Obadiah told Elijah that he had hidden one hundred prophets in caves. I Kings 18:13. Yet Elijah told the Lord that he was the only one left. "And I alone am left, and they seek my life, to take it away." I Kings19:10. When a Christian is on a pity trip logic is thrown out the window. Depression makes a person see things subjectively rather than objectively.

4. He lay down under a juniper tree and slept and ate, slept and ate, etc. People in deep depression have a greater demand for sleep than normal. They are tired because depression drains them of strength. I Kings 19:5-8. One of the ways to resist depression is bodily activity. When an emotion is in control, its nature will manifest symptoms that will keep it in control.

5. His self-confidence was at an all time low. When a believer's relationship with God is short-circuited it automatically casts a shadow over his spiritual abilities and relationship. When a believer doubts himself, it can be the direct result of doubting God. Elijah quickly lost confidence in God, because God did not act the way Elijah expected.

6. He withdrew from everyone. A natural tendency for those who are depressed is to remove themselves from society. The attitude of "They don't love me and won't miss me anyway," justifies isolation. If they are on a pity

trip, they will not pray for joy and peace. Instead they complain about their problems. They believe life has blind-sided them.

7. There was a desire to escape from his responsibility and even life itself. Elijah said "It is enough; now, 0 Lord, take my life, for I am not better than my fathers." I Kings 19:4. He had developed a martyr's complex. A focus on self had taken center stage in his life and not the desire to minister as a prophet of God to Israel.

8. He was oversensitive to Jezebel's threats. She could not have taken his life after these miracles, for fear of the people. Depressed people tend to be supersensitive to the caustic remarks of others. By heeding her threats he in effect made her his god, by believing she could harm his life, when God was his protector.

THE CAUSES OF ELIJAH'S DEPRESSION

He was spiritually depleted

After contesting with the forces of evil all day Elijah was spiritually depleted. A person is least alert after a significant spiritual victory. A Christian tends to allow pride and a sense of self-exaltation to take place after a great victory. Elijah's hopes had culminated, after years of waiting on God, at Mt. Carmel. He was on a spiritual high. After a mountain top experience there is usually a spiritual valley. Elijah prayed, after the fire fell from heaven, for rain. It took a simple prayer to call down fire from heaven, but he had to pray seven times for rain. After praying he was spiritually depleted. One may wonder about his thinking and his emotional state when he asked his servant seven different times to go look and see if anything was happening. Did his faith waver and this is why he prayed seven times?

The question, which needs to be asked, is, after this experience at Mt. Carmel did God want him to go to Jezreel? *"Then the hand of the Lord was on Elijah, and he girded up his loins and outran Ahab to*

Jezreel." I Kings 18:46. The answer would be yes or the hand of the Lord would not have empowered him to outrun Ahab's chariot. God had a reason for Elijah in Jezreel and it was not to flee to the wilderness. The question must be asked; Did God know that Elijah would run scared? The answer is yes. Elijah is an example for believers to watch their walk and relationship with God. However, Elijah could have discovered God's purpose for his life, had he waited on the Lord instead of fleeing in fear. Some of the greatest opportunities for believers to walk in faith and to minister are missed because of emotional conflicts.

He was physically exhausted

Elijah arrived at Jezreel physically exhausted. He had run in God's Spirit to Jezreel seventeen to twenty miles from Mt. Carmel. Elijah's exhaustion and emotions could have so blocked his mind that he was unable to see things spiritually. Because of fear, he *"ran for his life,"* to Beersheba ninety miles away. I Kings 9:3. Then, he went another day's journey into the wilderness. Physical exhaustion was a large part of his despair and desire to die. The Lord prepared the body in such a way that it needs rests. Even Christians are human. When Jesus was on earth, He relegated His life to the same needs of mankind. He had to eat and sleep. Christians are not expected to be supermen.

He had unfulfilled expectations

As has been mentioned, unfulfilled expectations were a part of his loss of faith. For three and one-half years he had imagined and perhaps drooled over what God would do. Fire fell from heaven and rain came because of his prayers. He was so excited, he ran to Jezreel to see what God would do. Apparently God had no plans to eliminate Ahab and Jezebel. He may have thought "Why did I waste three and one half years if God was not going to destroy them or at least Jezebel?" It is evident to me that God did not measure up to Elijah's expectations. Christians need to die to their expectations and learn to seek and find God's purpose or will.

He had emotional conflicts

Elijah allowed his emotions to control his actions. This emotional conflict is seen when he allowed fear to control his actions. I Kings 19:3. *"...and he was afraid and arose and ran for his life."* Fear replaced faith. He was engulfed with doubt and despair. He was so disappointed he wanted to die. This happens when a believer is in deep depression like Elijah. Depression is a combination of many emotions moving together in a coordinated attack on the spiritual man. Paul wrote, *"For the flesh sets its desire against the Spirit and the Spirit against the flesh; for these are in opposition to one another, so that you may not do the things that you please."* Galatians 5:17.

He was spiritually oppressed

The final cause to be explored is spiritual oppression. Jezebel's attack on Elijah is a type of demonic attack or spiritual warfare. She threatened his life. A threat of an attack is often more successful than an attack. Satan enjoys throwing fiery darts at believers. The evil one usually attacks through the agency of other humans, who are his pawns. Believers who have a spiritual mission or a God-directed ministry are more likely to be attacked. Elijah had been used by the Lord to destroy the works of the devil, so he came under attack. Satan has the ability to oppress the believer, using the emotions, through ground given him by the believer. Paul said, *"Be angry, and yet do not sin; do not let the sun go down upon your anger, and do not give the devil an opportunity."* Ephesians 4:26-27. The word *opportunity* in the Greek is *topos*, usually translated place. Prolonged anger gives the devil the place, ground or opportunity to wage war against the believer. Satan through Jezebel attacked Elijah indirectly and he won the skirmish. However, God always wins the battle. Remember, the joy of the Lord is the opposite of depression.

THE CURE FOR ELIJAH'S DEPRESSION

The Lord brought Elijah to Mt. Horeb or Sinai. Horeb means, *"the waste."* Forty days and nights, he wandered. The distance was no more than thirty or forty miles from the juniper tree in the wilderness. Why didn't God take him immediately to Horeb? This reveals God allows believers to suffer in depression until they are ready to be released. Believers are usually depressed because they choose to be depressed. What happened when Elijah had an encounter with the Lord?

A reassessment of his spiritual position

The Lord asked the question, *"What are you doing here Elijah?"* I Kings 19:13. The Lord's desire for Elijah was to get over his pity party. Elijah must have been anticipating something remarkable, since the Spirit led him for forty days. When the question was posed, he was still in the midst of self-pity. The true answer would have been, "I am here to meet with you. You are in charge. What do you desire that your servant do?" By asking the question, God wanted Elijah to recognize His sovereignty and become a submissive servant. Elijah's response to the question was self-exalting. He said, "*I have been very zealous for the Lord.*"

It also revealed self-pity, "*I alone am left and they seek my life to take it away.*" I Kings 19:10. The fact that Jezebel desired to kill him was nothing new, since he was a wanted man for three years. I Kings 18:10. Ahab had looked for him for years. Elijah's response is typical of those who are in deep depression. They look at life from a subjective point of view and seldom see the positive. Life is centered around self and not on God's word or work.

A reassurance of God's power

The Lord led the prophet to the mountain to reassure him of His sovereign power. The Lord told Elijah, "*Go forth, and stand on the mountain before the Lord.*" I Kings 19:11. God revealed His power through nature. In essence God communicated to Elijah that if He could control the wind, earthquakes and fire, He surely could control men. This revealed the absolute sovereignty of God over all things. After each of these miraculous events of nature the word states, "*the Lord was not in.*" God needed to get Elijah's mind and emotions refocused on His sovereignty and used these elements in an attempt to get his attention. Even after God revealed His power, Elijah was still cloaked in his self-pity. It appears miraculous works did not phase the prophet. It is the same for some people who are in a state of self-pity. They cannot see the obvious work or hand of God in things.

A second reassessment of his spiritual position

The Lord asked Elijah two times, "*What are you doing here, Elijah?*" The Lord asked the question when he arrived at the cave and again after three miraculous happenings. Elijah's reason and response were the same even after witnessing the miracles. He had not received the message. However, Elijah showed reverence and respect when "*...he wrapped his face in his mantle, and went out and stood in the entrance of the cave.*" This revealed humility and a reverence for God. Elijah did recognize the holiness and power of God. His attitude, in the midst of spiritual bankruptcy was respect and honor. God allowed Elijah time to wallow in his self-pity for forty days. Then it appears God was saying "Are you certain you know what you are doing? Do you really know who I am? Are you ready and willing to be my servant?" What is not written is as important as what is written. Apparently Elijah realized his mistakes, since God gave him some assignments.

A reassignment to a spiritual position

Elijah was recommissioned to a ministry task. He retained his position as a prophet of the Lord. It is reassuring to know God is not finished with His children, even when they blow it big time. However, it seems God was saying, "Enough is enough, get up and go to work." He did say *"Go return on your way to the wilderness of Damascus."* The message God probably communicated to Elijah was, "There is work to be done. Get your mind off yourself and on My mission. Life is bigger than you. Get a new perspective. My plan is laid out. Here is what I want you to do. Things are working out the way I purpose them and you need to accept my sovereignty." In the process The Lord enlightened Elijah when He said, *"Yet I will leave 7,000 in all of Israel, all the knees that have not bowed to Baal and every mouth that has not kissed him."* I Kings 19:18. These were believers who were faithful. God was saying to Elijah "You are not alone and I know what is going on." It was as if God said to Elijah "So you goofed, that doesn't make you unusable; get up and go to work." To fail does not make one a failure. Believers often need reassurance in their ministries. As God gave reassurance to Elijah after his cowardly actions, so he will give reassurance to believers who fail.

Real Life Illustration

A lady who was a member of a church, which I pastored, came in for counseling. She was in deep depression. Her marriage was not living up to her expectations. She said she would be happy if her husband was different. When asked what she expected of her husband, she responded with five items. One of the items was she wanted him to be saved. Another was to begin attending church. In a few months all five of her expectations came to reality. A short time after his salvation she returned indicating she was so unhappy. I asked her what was the problem and she indicated it was her husband. During the session she had five different expectations. She was reminded of the five expectations in the first session and her reply was, I know but this is what I really want him to do. Needless to say she never faced the problem, which lay within. She and her expectations were the problem.

Verbal Commitment to the Lord

Repeat the following to another person, I know that depression is not a sin unless I allow it to control my life. It is a natural emotion. However, it is one area that Satan uses to defeat believers. I recognize that depression can be resisted and through praising God, depression will go away, unless it is a chemical imbalance. Depression, like anger is a God-given emotion, handled rightly is for our good. However, it can bring spiritual defeat. Allowing it to dominate over an extended period of time reveals a lack of faith. It also shows the flesh is in control, not the Holy Spirit. It causes Christians to lose their vision of God's work. Based on this I choose to praise God in all things. I accept the fact that nothing is happening in my life, which has caught God off guard. He knew what would happen prior to it happening. He will cause things to work out for good. I refuse to be down when God says things are okay. I will continue addressing this emotion by continually praising God. This reveals faith not unbelief. I recognize joy is the opposite of depression. When I feel depressed, I will begin claiming the joy of the Lord.

Thought Provoking Questions

1. Is depression a normal part of your emotional reaction to pressures? Is it controllable? Is depression a sin?

2. Since depression is a focus of the flesh and not of the Spirit, when does it become a sin to be depressed?

3. Depression can come upon a Christian as a result of demonic oppression. What can be done to resist these attacks?

4. What are some positive ways a believer can get out of self-pity doldrums?

5. Is depression an outward sign of doubt and a lack of faith?

† Warfare Prayer

Father, I confess depression is the result of self-pity or an attack by the forces of evil. I praise You for (the incident or occasion which caused depression), and ask that your joy would fill my life. I know that continuous praise will lift the garment of heaviness. I ask that any oppressive power of the enemy be broken. If I have given the enemy any ground to wage war against me, I ask that this would be revealed to me, so I can have victory over the enemy. I ask the Holy Spirit to remind me of anything that has occurred in the past, which enable depression to have a root in my life. I ask that these previous thoughts and events be robbed of their power to influence my emotions. Depression is the enemy of a faith walk. To be continually depressed is elevating self above God. It is a focus on the flesh. I choose to walk by the Spirit, so that I will not do the deeds of the flesh. I recognize depression can be a chemical imbalance, but most of the time it comes from self or the forces of evil. I pray for You to enlighten me when I begin to feel depressed. It is my desire for you to be glorified and worshiped.

STEPS OF ACTION

- Accept the fact that depression is part of the normal emotional reaction of believers, which can be controlled.

- Excessive depression is an extreme focus on self; therefore, when it raises its ugly head in this manner deny it. Look for ways to assist others. If possible find someone with greater trials or problems than yours. Begin to pray for them, while praising God for your problems.

- Do not allow depression to keep you in bed or moping inside. Make a point of dressing up; engage in some outside activity or exercise.

- Think with an attitude of faith. Depression is often a result of unfulfilled expectations, which results in self-pity. Therefore, praise the Lord each day for every circumstance. Joy comes as a result of praise and gratefulness. Joy is the opposite of depression. Praise, confess and sing away depression.

- Depression may come as a result of demonic attack. This demands submission to God. Then resist the devil and he will flee from you. If submitting to the Lord and praising Him in all things do not lift depression, then it is a chemical imbalance. Make an appointment with a doctor.

Chapter 5

The Key to Controlling Resentment
Matthew 18:21-35

The following are a few questions, which need to be answered before a believer begins this study. Be honest and answer each question without supposing what God would have you write.

1. Is there anyone you hate or resent?

2. Has anyone harmed or hurt you and you are unwilling to forgive them?

3. When you recall past events, is there anything, which creates anger or hatred or affects you in a negative way?

4. Do you blame God for anything?

5. Do you ever use mental thoughts, which are intended to inflict pain on someone without their knowledge?

Introduction

Resentment motivates the emotions to act contrary to the love and grace of God. Resentment is held on to and cherished, as one would do with a lover. It is the one sin, which separates a believer from the presence of the Holy Spirit. Jesus said, *"But if you do not forgive men, then your Father will not forgive your transgressions."* Matthew 6:15. Some Christians interpret this statement as a person losing his or her salvation. However, it is losing fellowship with God. Remember, when a believer is born again ever sin past present and future is forgiven regarding an eternal relationship with God. Christians have an earthly relationship as well as an eternal relationship. This earthly relationship requires a believer to repent and to forgive. This principle will be explained in this chapter.

> **Text:** *"Then Peter came and said to Him, 'Lord, how often shall my brother sin against me and I forgive him? Up to seven times?' Jesus said to him, 'I do not say to you, seven times, but up to seventy times seven. For this reason the kingdom may be compared to a certain king who wished to settle accounts with his slaves. And when he had begun to settle them, there was brought to him one who owed him ten thousand talents. But since he did not have the means to repay, his lord commanded him to be sold, along with his wife and children and all that he had, and repayment to be made. The slave therefore falling down, prostrated himself before him, saying 'Have patience with me, and I will repay you everything.' And the Lord of that slave felt compassion and released him and forgave him the debt. But that slave went out and found one of his fellow slaves who owed him a hundred denarii; and he seized him and began to choke him, saying, 'Pay back what you owe.' So his fellow slave fell down and began to entreat him, saying, 'Have patience with me and I will repay you'. He was unwilling however, but went and threw him in prison until he should pay back what was owed. So when his fellow slaves saw what had happened, they were deeply grieved and came and reported to their Lord all that had happened. Then summoning him, his lord said to him, 'You wicked slave; I forgave you all that debt because you entreated me. Should you not also have had mercy on your fellow slave, even as I had mercy on you? And his lord, moved with anger, handed him over to the torturers until he should repay all that was owed him. So shall My heavenly Father also do to you, if each of you does not forgive his brother from your heart." Matthew 18:21-35*

The Descriptions of Resentment

THE DEFINITIONS OF RESENTMENT

Resentment is yesterday's anger etched into the mind and emotions. The hurts, insults, wrongs, real or imagined of the past, which have developed into today's resentments. The wrongs are mulled over in the mind, usually with the offender receiving a justifiable punishment. Everyone has cause to resent and has resented others. Resentment is a part of the fleshly nature. Usually the greater the negative opinion of self, greater is the resentment. Resentment is the offended exacting punishment on the offender, overtly or covertly. This resentment may be shown by silence, violence, slander, coolness aloofness, and unfriendliness to name a few of the expressed attitudes.

Why are hurts, insults, and wrongs remembered? Why is the hurt prolonged by the mind? Why do the emotions take a wrong and make a mountain out of a molehill? Emotions justify resentment of a wrong suffered. Resentment is accepting the premise, "Vengeance is mine I will repay, says the offended." Resentment clouds ones thinking, and blinds a person to the character of others. Resentment is accepting the performance of a person, as that person, and then resenting his person as well as his performance. This is not the attitude of love God displays toward mankind. He separates a person, after salvation, from his actions. He can love the person and hate his performance or sins. Resentment goes contrary to love as described in I Corinthians 13:5, *"Love does not take into account a wrong suffered."* Resentment does take into account a wrong suffered. Resentment keeps a ledger book on wrongs. In counseling, the greatest liability for a good marriage is the past wrongs dredged up to justify a person's anger.

Again be reminded resentment is yesterday's anger etched into the minds and emotions. It is woven together so tightly in the emotions it affects relationships with others. This anger simmers inside until some incident awakens it and it boils forth. Time does not dilute resentment; rather it grows stronger until it manifests itself in some emotional reaction. Resentment also is the offended exacting punishment on the offender for a real or imaginary offense. The exacting of punishment may take many forms. It may be expressed through anger, sarcasm, carping, accusations, and a host of other expressions. It may involve an overt act of revenge. Some people have attempted to punish others by puncturing tires, damaging homes and one man unloaded his cement truck in another man's convertible. Resentment is to feel or express disdain or indignant displeasure. Webster defines it as, "A feeling of indignant displeasure because of something regarded as a wrong or insult." It is to take into account a wrong suffered. I Corinthians 13:5. This is holding a grudge. Resentment is holding the offender's feet to the fire. It is keeping a ledger book on offenses. In an argument, it is throwing into the face of a mate something dredged up after years have gone by.

THE DANGERS OF RESENTMENT

Resentment robs one of joy

A resentful Christian is an ungrateful person. He cannot praise God for the wrong done to him. This ungratefulness steals his joy, since joy is the outgrowth of gratefulness. If joy is lacking in your life jump ahead and read Chapter 10. Life comes by God's grace. Grace means something is undeserved or unmerited; it is a gift. In order to destroy resentment a believer must praise God for the situation, which results in joy. In the Sermon on the Mount, Jesus said *"But I say to you, love your enemies, and pray for those who persecute you."* This command by the Lord, if followed, short-circuits resentment. Paul instructed the Philippians to rejoice in all things. *"Rejoice in the Lord always; again I say rejoice."* Philippians 4:4.

In addition resentment is unforgiveness. Jesus indicated if we did not forgive, neither would we be forgiven. This does not mean a Christian would not be saved, but it does mean they will be out of fellowship with the Lord. They cannot have joy when it is a fruit of the Spirit. More attention will be paid to this thought later in the chapter.

Resentment roots into bitterness

"See to it that no one comes short of the grace of God, that no root of bitterness springing up causes trouble, and by it many are defiled." Hebrews 12:15. Grace, as has been noted, is unmerited favor from God to man. Grace is also to be shown in interpersonal relationships. Paul wrote in Ephesians 4:29, *"Let no unwholesome word proceed from your mouth but only such a word as is good for edification according to the need of the moment, that it may give grace to those who hear."* Not only do believers receive grace they are to give grace. Anyone can give a good word when it is deserved. Grace is giving a good word when it is not deserved. Grace loves unconditionally. Resentment and bitterness can control a believer only if he is unwilling to forgive. Resentment always has a by-product and that is, its effect on others. This passage in Hebrews indicates that others are "defiled." "Defile" is to pollute, contaminate or soil. Uncontrolled resentment causes bitterness, which contaminates others causing them to sin. Bitterness in one believer may create bitterness in others, since the passage in Hebrews relates *"and by it many are defiled."*

Dignifying Resentment

RESENTMENT IS DIGNIFIED BY ONE'S PLEASURES IN IT

Dignifying resentment is shown by statements such as, "I would never do anything like that. I would never act like that. I have never hurt anyone this bad." This type of attitude shows disdain or a looking down one's nose at others. It is an attempt to justify self and put down another. The root sin is pride. The inner attitude is self-centeredness. One's ego places him or her in a spirit of condemnation in order to justify resentment. Counselors often hear this sort of statements, "I cannot forgive them, and you do not understand how bad they hurt me." No matter how deeply a person is hurt there can be no justification in retaining an attitude of unforgiveness. Resentment cultivates an attitude of revenge

The mind, acting on resentment, develops plots to take revenge on the offender. Often, it imagines some tragic accident-taking place, always with the idea of the offender being punished. As part of revenge, the offended usually withholds friendship, displays a coldness, etc. Paul wrote in Romans 12:19, *"Never take your own revenge, beloved, but leave room for the wrath of God, for it is written, 'Vengeance is Mine, I will repay,' says the Lord."* As one plots inwardly, there is an inner satisfaction with the possibilities of hurting the offender. This type of mental gymnastics does not remove the resentment. In most cases, resentments are compounded.

RESENTMENT IS DIGNIFIED BY ONE'S PROTECTION OF IT

The attitude of, "I have every right to be angry for what they did to me," illustrates self-justification. Nothing justifies resentment. "I am not hurting anyone with my feelings," is another statement to justify resenting the offender. However, resentment cannot be hidden and is openly projected to others. This will involve others choosing sides. A believer, to be in God's will, must forgive. Jesus made this clear in Matthew 6:15, *"But if you do not forgive men, then your Father will not forgive your transgressions."* Resentment is protected by an attitude of unforgiveness. The offended, to resent, has to be unwilling to forgive. To be forgiven by the offender is the offenders will not be punished for their actions. Deep hurt is used as a cover-up for failing to forgive. Forgiveness is the offended bearing the offenses of the offender and allowing the offender to be free from punishment by the offended. It is a picture of grace and mercy. It is love displayed through the cross.

RESENTMENT IS DIGNIFIED BY ONE'S PRACTICE OF IT

Resentment practices a rebellion to authority

A person who resents goes contrary to God's command to forgive. A willful disobedience to God's command is outright rebellion. This is as the sin of witchcraft, according to I Samuel 15:23, *"For rebellion is as the sin of divination* [the practice of witchcraft] *and insubordination is as iniquity and idolatry."* Jesus commanded forgiveness as recorded in Matthew 6:15. *"But if you do not forgive men, then your Father will not forgive your transgression."* Jesus gave a parable to illustrate forgiveness. At the conclusion of the parable Jesus said, *"And his Lord moved with anger, handed him over to the torturers until he should repay all that was owed him. So shall My heavenly Father also do to you, if each of you does not forgive his brother from your heart."* Matthew 18:34-35. The torturers were the jailers. Jesus was not saying that unforgiveness would send one to hell. As the servant was turned over to the torturers or jailers, believers with an attitude of unforgiveness would be turned over to the torturers. The spiritual understanding would be an unforgiving believer would be turned over to the wicked ones. Paul alluded to this possibility in his letter to Corinth. He wrote, *"I have decided to deliver such a one to Satan for the destruction of his flesh, that his spirit may be saved in the day of the Lord Jesus."* 1 Corinthians 5:5.

Resentment practices a resistance to reconciliation

It causes a rift in Christian fellowship involving others. The attitude is, "I don't want to even see them, much less talk to them. When they prove they are truly sorry, I may be willing to talk to them." This is forgiveness with a hook. It is an attitude, "If they crawl, or are penitent enough, maybe I will forgive." Another of Jesus' parables illustrated this attitude. In the parable of the prodigal son, the older brother displayed resentment. His father, pleaded with him to enter the house and reconcile with his brother and he refused. Most church splits are the result of resentment. Believers hold each other's feet to the fire, and refuse to reconcile. This is the opposite of what the Lord commanded. When Peter asked, *"Lord, how often shall my brother sin against me and I forgive him? Up to seven times? Jesus said to him, 'I do not say to you, up to seven times, but up to seventy times seven.'"* Matthew 18:21-22. This statement by Jesus means an unlimited number of times. There should be no room for resentment in the Christian's heart.

Resentment practices a restricted reasoning ability

Emotions tend to cloud the mind. A resentful person is subjective about an offender and does not see the offender from an objective frame of mind. He is unable to see the offender's real character, goodness, abilities, or needs. He is blinded by resentment. When forgiveness comes, the offender can become the best friend of the offended. This is true of the believer with God. In marital conflicts resentment looks at a few negative character qualities and overlooks the many positive qualities of the other mate. Resentment is an inward look focused on self and not looking outwardly in an objective manner toward others. The older brother in the parable of the prodigal son illustrates this type of reasoning. The younger brother had repented, and desired to be nothing more than a servant of the father. He told his father, *"Father, I have sinned against heaven and in your sight; I am no longer worthy to be called your son."* Luke 15:21. The older brother out of resentment said, *"...when this son of yours came who devoured your wealth with harlots, you killed the fatted calf for him."* Luke 15:30. He could not accept the father's judgement of his son's change of life.

The Demise of Resentment

The only solution to overcoming resentment is forgiveness. Forgiveness is easier to express when an offender manifests a contrite and repentant spirit, and asks for forgiveness. However, the Christian who is offended should forgive immediately after an offense, regardless of what the offender's attitude may be. This is done based on agape love.

THE METHOD OF FORGIVENESS
IS THROUGH THE CROSS

Grace settled all accounts at the cross

Jesus was the sacrifice for man. Jesus was the Lamb slain from the foundation of the world for man's sins. He became the sin bearer. He was made to be sin. God's holy nature required that sin be punished. The underneath side of Gods holiness is His wrath toward sin. The very nature of holiness demands the punishment of sin. Jesus paid the price to redeem men from sin. God required a perfect sacrifice for sin; since man is imperfect, he could not pay for his own sin. It required the sacrifice of a perfect life, the Lord Jesus Christ. Jesus was the substitute for man. His being a substitute means He took man's place. He was punished on man's behalf. He paid the penalty in order that man could receive the forgiveness of sins." Sin condemns and the Bible indicates, *"That all have sinned and fall short of the glory of God."* Romans 3:23. Paul writes, *"For the wages of sin is* (eternal) *death, but the free gift of God is eternal life in Christ Jesus our Lord."* Romans 6:23. Jesus came down from heaven and became man so that He could live a perfect life as man. This would allow Him to give His life for man. Eternal life is conditional; it requires an exchanged life. Since He gave His life for believers, believers are required to give Him their life.

Grace settles all accounts through the cross

Christians are sinners *"saved by grace."* They are saved from the past, present and future sins. Christians are brought into a new relationship, a relationship of forgiveness. *"And be kind to one another, tenderhearted, forgiving each other, just as God in Christ also has forgiven you."* Ephesians 4:32. *Peter asked Jesus, "Lord, how often shall my brother sin against me and I forgive him? Up to seven times. Jesus said to him, I do not say to you, up to seven times, but up to seventy time seven."* Matthew 18:21. In the text Jesus gave a parable describing a slave that was forgiven a debt of millions of dollars in today's money, who would not in return forgive a fellow slave who owed him a few hundred dollars. When God forgives believers it is for a tremendous amount of sin, and they are obligated to forgive a fellow believer for a few small offences.

THE MEANING OF FORGIVENESS

The description of forgiveness

Forgiveness is the offended bearing the offense or wrong of the offender and allowing the offender to be free from the wrong. This is what Jesus did for mankind. He bore the penalty for man's sin and allowed man to be free from punishment. Forgiveness does not demand explanations or apologies. Forgiveness does not need to clear up all misunderstandings. Forgiveness releases a Christian from resentment of yesterday's wrongs. Forgiveness allows the past to die, accounts to go unsettled, differences to remain unsolved, ledger books to be erased or to stay unbalanced. Forgiveness believes that anything done to a believer is done to the Lord. It is allowing God to battle on your behalf.

The demand for forgiveness

The demand of forgiveness is seen in the text. Remember the above quotation where Jesus said to Peter, *"I do not say to you, up to seven times, but up to seventy times seven."* Jesus places forgiveness in a new light for the disciples. He states that a believer should forgive an unlimited number of times for the same kind of offense. Jesus related to His disciples a parable regarding forgiveness as recorded in Matthew 18:21-35. This parable came as a result of Peter's question regarding forgiveness. Peter asked, *"Lord, how often shall my brother sin against me and I forgive him? Up to seven times?"* The final conclusion of this parable is found in verses 34 and 35, *"And his Lord, moved with anger, handed him over to the torturers until he should repay all that was owed him. So shall My heavenly Father also do to you, if each of you do not forgive his brother form your heart."* As has been noted previously, Jesus is not indicating believers would be lost after being saved. It does indicate the removal of His protection and allows the forces of evil to attack. The torturers in this parable do not represent hell; the jail represents oppression by the enemy of Christians, the devil. Remember what Paul said about the man living in immorality at Corinth. He wrote, *"For I, on my part, though absent in body but present in spirit, have already judged him who has so committed this, as though I were present...I have decided to deliver such a one to Satan for the destruction of the flesh, that his spirit may be saved in the day of the Lord Jesus."* I Corinthians 5:3,5. Unforgiveness also limits fellowship with the Lord. In I John 2:11, John describes unforgiveness, *"But the one who hates his brother is in darkness and walks in darkness, and does not know where he is going because the darkness has blinded his eyes."* In chapter 4 of this epistle, John wrote, *"If someone says, I love God and hates his brother, he is a liar."* Unforgiveness and love are not synonyms. However, love and forgiveness are synonyms. The Father demands that believers forgive.

Chapter seven will illustrate forgiveness using Luke 15, which contains the parable of the Prodigal son. If needed read this chapter and return to go through the heart searcher at the end of this chapter.

Real Life Illustration

In a former church one of the leaders had an obvious problem with me. The resentment was apparent. I could not imagine the cause of the resentment. One day he confronted me about the problem and indicated it began about a year ago. He thought I had married a couple that had multiple marriages. When it was told to him that this was not true, his response was "Well I thought you did." Resentment can arise out of someone's failure to live up to someone else's expectations.

Verbal Commitment to the Lord

Repeat the following to another person, I know the Lord forgave me of all of my sins. I also know I did not deserve His forgiveness. It was by His grace. I choose to give grace to others by forgiving. It does not matter the amount of harm and sin, which has been directed toward me. It is minute compared to the sins I have committed against God. He forgave me and I choose to forgive. I will not allow anything to separate me from fellowship with God. An unforgiving attitude results in losing fellowship with God. Jesus said, *"For if you forgive men for their transgressions, your heavenly Father will also forgive you. But if you do not forgive men, then your Father will not forgive your transgression."* Matthew 6:14-15. I recognize His unforgiveness is not losing one's salvation, but rather it is a loss of fellowship. I choose to forgive, no matter what.

Real Life Illustration

I've had numerous experiences counseling believers with a resentful spirit. A twenty-one-year-old lady who had been in clinical care for five years had a problem with agoraphobia. She was set free from this emotional malady by confessing the sin of resentment. She had resented her father for divorcing her mother, leaving the family, and taking up with another woman. This resentment developed into bitterness. The wicked one used this as a wedge to work on the emotional person. As a result of confessing the resentment, and determining to forgive and love her father, confession removed the basis for which Satan could use in his attack. Resentment is hidden anger. Note what Paul wrote to the Ephesians, *"Be angry, and yet do not sin; do not let the sun go down on your anger, and do not give the devil an opportunity."* Ephesians 4:27-28. The word *opportunity* in the Greek is *topas*, which is literally, place.

Thought Provoking Questions

1. Which of the following statements reveal resentment? Circle the ones, which apply.

   a. I hold a grudge against my mother-in-law.

   b. I hate that man because of what he did to me.

   c. I am not going to forgive that person because of what he did to me.

   d. I was raped and he hasn't asked for forgiveness so I detest him?

2. Is there anything that can be done to a Christian, in which resentment is justified?

3. Do you have to forgive another person, if they do not ask for forgiveness?

4. Does resentment and unforgiveness reveal a root sin of pride?

5. Why is it when believers fail to forgive that it gives the evil forces an opportunity to attach a Christian?

6. Can a believer be submitted to God and hold resentment against another believer?

7. If a believer has resentment toward others and resists the devil, will he flee?

† **Warfare Prayer**

Father I confess the sin of resentment toward (name of person or persons including God.) I ask the Holy Spirit to reveal to me the reasons for the resentment so that I can confess any sin connected with it. I acknowledge that if I fail to forgive, I will not be forgiven and will be out of fellowship with You. I ask with an attitude of repentance and make David's prayer, my prayer, "*Wash me throughly from my iniquity, and cleanse me from my sin.*" I know that a failure to forgive leads to bitterness and thus causes all types of evil. It is evident from the fore-mentioned parable that a failure to forgive gives Satan an unfettered attack on me. If I fail to forgive, I am not submitted to You and the devil does not have to flee. Any resentment toward self, parents, friends, neighbors, employers, and fellow employees, I confess and ask for forgiveness. This also includes any and all sin of resentment toward You. I remember a failure to accept myself, as your creation is to resent You as creator. I do accept all that You have done and are currently doing in and through my life. I am fully submitted to You, the Lord of the universe and the Lord of my life. It is my desire to be set free from the power of evil. Anything, which has occurred in the past, which gives power to the enemy, I ask You to bring it to remembrance so I can confess it.

STEPS OF ACTION

- Ask yourself the following questions and be ready to forgive. Is there anyone against whom I hold a grudge? Is there anyone I have not forgiven? Is there anyone I hate? Is there anyone I do not love? Are there any misunderstandings I am unwilling to forget? Is there any person against whom I am harboring bitterness or resentment? Is there anyone I dislike to hear praised or exalted? Do I allow anything to justify a wrong attitude toward others? Do I have a disposition to resent and retaliate when disapproved of or contradicted?

- If the answer to any of the above questions is yes, write down each of the names and incidents, which caused resentment. Note: writing things down provides the Holy Spirit an opportunity to remind you of people you need to forgive or events you need to forget. Remember, forgiveness is an act of faith, and the emotions may not feel like forgiving. Continue acting in faith by forgiving, until the emotions come into harmony with the leadership of God's Spirit.

- Declare aloud as often as needed that emotions will not control my faith life in the matter of forgiving.

- If your resentment is directed toward God because of a loss of a loved one, an injustice done to you, loss of a job, health problems or a myriad of other reasons, confess the resentment and ask God to fill you with His Holy Spirit.

- The following exercise is what was asked of the young lady, illustrated in Real Life Experiences listed previously. Use a paper and carefully work through the following questions, allowing the Holy Spirit to point out sins, which need to be confessed. Write them down, confess them to the Lord and destroy the paper as a sign of God's forgiveness and cleansing.

The following is called the heart searcher. I acquired these questions in the early 1970's from an anonymous author. The following questions have assisted many people over the years to live a godly life. I trust you will read them carefully and be honest with the Lord about any sin in which He convicts.

The scriptural basis for confession of sin, "*How blessed is he whose transgression is forgiven, whose sin is covered! How blessed is the man to whom the Lord does not impute iniquity, and in whose spirit there is no deceit! When I kept silent about my sin, my body wasted away through groaning all day long. For day and night Thy hand was heavy upon me; my vitality was drained away as with the fever heat of summer. I acknowledged my sin to Thee, and my iniquity I did not hide; I said, 'I will confess my transgressions to the Lord,' and Thou didst forgive the guilt of my sin.*" Psalm 32:1-5.

Remember confession of sin is necessary for fellowship with God and for reviving your spiritual life. In reading the following questions when you are convicted of sin, confess it at once, asking to be cleansed from the sin and the power it has had on your life. Take time to allow the Holy Spirit to reveal other connecting sins. After confessing, claim your cleansing and accept your forgiveness.

No matter what other believers may or may not do, a revived heart requires doing nothing that will go contrary to the inner leading of God's Spirit. You will have a cleansed life if you answer the questions truthfully and confess sin completely. It is very important to write down the sin or sins. It will assist you in remembering that the sin was confessed, when the wicked one accuses you later.

1. "If you forgive men for their transgressions, your heavenly Father will also forgive you. But if you do not forgive men, then your Father will not forgive your transgressions." Matthew. 6:14ff

   Is there anyone against whom you hold a grudge? Anyone you haven't forgiven? Is there any person you cannot love? Are there any misunderstandings that you are unwilling to forgive? Is there any person against whom you are harboring bitterness, resentment, or jealousy? Anyone you dislike to hear praised or well spoken of? Do you allow anything to justify a wrong attitude toward another person?

2. *"But seek first His kingdom and His righteousness; and all these things shall he added to you."* Matthew 6:33. Is there anything in which you have failed to put God first? Have your decisions been made after your own wisdom and desires rather than seeking and following God's will? Do any of the following, in any way, interfere with your surrender and service to God, ambition, pleasures, loved ones, friendships, desire for recognition, money, your own plans?

3. *"Go therefore and make disciples of all the nations, baptizing them in the name of the Father and the Son and the Holy Spirit."* Matthew 28:19. Have you failed to seek the lost for Christ? Have you failed to verbally witness consistently for the Lord Jesus Christ? Has your life not shown the Lord Jesus to the lost?

4. *"But if you have bitter jealousy and selfish ambition in your heart, do not be arrogant and so lie against the truth."* James 3:14. Are you secretly pleased over the misfortunes of another? Are you secretly annoyed over the accomplishments or advancements of another? Are you guilty of any contention or strife? Do you quarrel, argue, or engage in heated discussions? Are you a partaker in any divisions? Are there people whom you deliberately slight?

5. *"Will a man rob God? Yet you are robbing Me! But you say, 'How have we robbed Thee? In tithes and offerings."* Malachi 3:8. Have you robbed God by withholding His due of time, talents, and money? Have you given less than a tenth of your income for God's work? Have you failed to support mission work in prayer and in offerings?

6. *"And the Lord said, 'Who then is the faithful and sensible steward whom the master will put in charge of his servants, to give them their rations at the proper time? Blessed is that slave whom his master finds so doing when he comes."* Luke 12:42-43. Are you undependable, so that you cannot be trusted with responsibilities in the Lord's work? Are you allowing your emotions to be stirred for things of the Lord, but doing nothing about it?

7. *"Or do you not know that your body is the temple of the Holy Spirit who is in you, whom you have from God, and that you are not your own? For you have been bought with a price, therefore glorify God in your body."* I Corinthians 6:19-20. Are you guilty of intemperance in drugs, drinking, smoking or eating? Do you care for your

body, including the emotions and mind as a temple of the
Living God? Are you depressed over a long period of time?
Do you tend to live in a fantasy world?

8. *"Whether then you eat or drink or what-ever you do,
   do all to the glory of God"* I Corinthians 10:31. Do you
   talk about what you have done, rather than talking about
   what Christ is doing? Do you take credit for anything
   good about yourself, rather than give all the glory to God?
   Are your statements mostly about "I"? Are your feelings
   easily hurt? Have you made a pretense of being something
   that you are not? Do you lie about places you have been
   and things you have done to impress others?

9. *I have been crucified with Christ; and it is no longer I
   who live, hut Christ lives in me; and the life which I now
   live in the flesh I live by faith in the Son of God who
   loved me, and delivered Himself up for me."* Galatians
   2:20. Are you self-conscious rather than Christ-conscious?
   Do you allow self to control your actions rather than the
   Spirit of God? Do you allow feelings of inferiority to keep
   you from attempting things you should in serving God?
   Remember, Paul wrote *'I can do all things through Him
   who strengthens me."* Philippians 4:13.

10. *"Let him who steals, steal no longer; but rather let
    him labor, performing with his own hands what is
    good, in order that he may have something to share
    with him who has need." Ephesians 4:28.* Do you do
    as little as you can get by with at work? Do you under
    pay your employees? Have you been careless in the
    payment of your debts? Have you sought some ungodly
    way of not paying legitimate debts? Do you waste
    the time of others? Are you lazy? Do you rob God by
    failing to give 10% of your income to Him?

11. *"Let all bitterness and wrath and anger and clamor and
    slander be put away from you, along with all malice."
    Ephesians 4:31.* Do you have a critical attitude toward

others? Do you complain and find fault? Would others accuse you of being irritable or cranky? Do you explode over minor things? Are you still angry over something, which happened sometime in the past? Are you harsh and unkind? Are you impatient with others? Is there anyone when brought to the mind, creates a rising negative emotion, such as resentment, fear, anger etc.?

12. *"Therefore be careful how you walk, not as unwise men, but as wise, making the most of your time, because the days are evil." Ephesians 5:15-16.* Do you listen to unedifying radio or TV programs? Do you read unworthy magazines? Do you participate in worldly amusements? Do you find it necessary to seek satisfaction from any questionable source? Are you doing and saying certain things, which show you are not satisfied in the Lord?

13. *"... always giving thanks for all things in the name of our Lord Jesus Christ to God, even the Father."* Ephesians 5:20. Have you neglected to thank Him, in the name of the Lord, for all things, the seemingly bad, as well as the good? Have you virtually called God a liar by believing He cannot cause all things to work together for good? Do you disbelieve God's word in attitudes and practice? Are you anxious and worried about life's problems? Is your spiritual temperament based on feelings instead of God's promises?

14. *"For to me, to live is Christ, and to die is gain."* Philippians *1:21.* Does anything mean more to you than living for and pleasing the Lord? Are you so involved in the cares of life that you do not have time for God? Does your daily conversation focus on the things of this life, rather than upon the Lord? Do you place self on the throne of your life, rather than the Lord? Do you live a daily life of faith, accepting all circumstances but not knowing the final results?

15. *"Do all things without grumbling or disputing, that you may prove yourselves to he blameless and innocent children of God, above reproach in the midst of a*

crooked and perverse generation, among whom you appear as lights in the world." Philippians 2:14-15. Do you ever, by word or deed, seek to hurt someone? Do you gossip? Do you speak unkindly concerning people when they are not present? Are you considered by others to be a complainer? Do you invariably grumble and complain about ministry activities?

16. *"Rejoice in the Lord always, again I will say rejoice."* *Philippians 4:4.* Do you have any resentment toward the Lord because of past circumstances or problems? Have you complained to others about how you think God is treating you? Have you been dissatisfied with His provision for your perceived needs? Have you deliberately disobeyed what you knew to be His will? Do you have any reservations regarding anything God may ask you to do?

17. *"Do not lie to one another, since you laid aside the old self with its evil practices."* *Colossians 3:9.* Do you ever lie? Do you tend to exaggerate? Do you steal? Do you cheat on your taxes? Do you take things from your work without paying for them and pass it off as perks? Do you give a full day's work for a full day's pay? Do you overcharge for items?

18. *"Now flee from youthful lusts, and pursue righteousness, faith, love and peace, with those who call on the Lord from a pure heart."* *2 Timothy 2:22.* Do you allow impure thoughts about the opposite sex to linger in your mind? Do you daydream about some person or persons in an intimate manner, knowing it is not godly? Do you read books or magazines that are impure or suggests unholy behavior? Do you indulge in any entertainment that is ungodly?

19. *"Not forsaking our own assembling together, as is the habit of some, but encouraging one another; and all the more, as you see the day drawing near."* *Hebrews 10:25.* Do you make any excuse to keep away from the

preaching and teaching of God's word? Do you ignore and do not attend meetings for prayer? Do you despise daily devotions? When others are praising the Lord, does this upset you? Do you thank the Lord for His daily provisions? Do you have a quiet time with the Lord?

20. *"Obey your leaders, and submit to them; for they keep watch over your souls, as those who will give an account."* Hebrews 13:17. Do you in any way have a stubborn or unteachable spirit? Do you willingly submit to the leaders in the church? Do you rebel at requests to help in the work of the gospel? Have you dishonored the Lord and hindered His work by criticizing His leaders? Have you failed to pray regularly for your pastor and staff?

IF YOU HAVE BEEN OPEN AND HONEST IN THE MATTER OF ADMITTING YOUR SINS, THEN YOU HAVE RECEIVED GOD'S CLEANSING.

REMEMBER:

1. If the sin is against God, confess it to God and accept His forgiveness.

2. If the sin is against another person, confess it to God and ask the person for forgiveness.

3. If the sin is against a group, confess it to God, and ask the group for forgiveness.

4. When every sin is confessed, accept your cleansing and cease holding your feet to the fire for the sin or sins. In other words forgive yourself, since God has forgiven you. If you cannot forgive yourself, then you are acting as God in your own life and need to confess the sin of idolatry. In effect, you are acting as your own god.

Chapter 6

❧

Control Anger, Become A Grace Giver

Ephesians 4:26-32

The following are a few questions, which need to be answered before a believer begins this study. Be honest and answer each question without supposing what God would have you write.

1. Would family members consider you as an angry person?

2. Do you ever throw a tempter tantrum and have difficulty saying I am sorry?

3. Do you believe anger can be controlled?

4. When do you think anger becomes a sin?

5. Can you remember the first time you were angry? What was the cause?

Introduction

Throughout the Bible, the righteous anger of God is expressed. God's wrath is an expression of His holiness. God's holy nature demands wrath against sin. He poured out His wrath on sin through the cross. The cross and hell reveal the depth of God's wrath against sin. Anger is one of God's emotional characteristics. However, unlike most of humanity, God is able to separate a sinner from his performance. He can hate sin and love the sinner. Anger, with man, begins with the thought process. Usually an angry person has allowed anger over the years to build a stronghold in the mind. An angry man becomes angry because he has an anger problem.

Anger is an inward reaction to some external force. Outside pressure does not create anger; it stirs up the inward anger already in existence. Anger is an inward emotion, often expressed outwardly. It is a wholesome emotion until it becomes a controlling force. Anger, when carried to the extreme, is rooted into pride and self-centeredness. When anger controls your actions and attitudes, this constitutes sin. This always displeases God. Anger declares war against God because it appeases the flesh. God's standard for believers is to be grace givers. Grace giving is allowing the grace of God to flow through the believer to others. It is a deliberate choice, by the believer, to act like Jesus. It is choosing not to hold grudges or resentment. It is forgiving, as an act of love. Anger expressed in hatred, resentment or bitterness expresses unbelief in God's ability to rectify the problem. It also reveals a rebellion against God's love. I have heard many Christians defend their anger problem, by stating "That's the way I am. People must accept me, since God made me this way." This passage refutes this type of thinking. Christians must learn to control their emotional outbursts of anger and the resulting resentment and bitterness.

> **Text:** *Be angry, and yet do not sin; do not let the sun go down on your anger, and do not give the devil an opportunity ... Let no unwholesome word proceed from your mouth, but only such a word as is good for edification according to the need of the moment, that it may give grace to those who hear. And do not grieve the Holy Spirit of God, by whom you were sealed for the day of redemption. Let all bitterness and wrath and anger and clamor and slander be put away from you, along with all malice. And be kind to one another, tenderhearted, forgiving each other, just as God in Christ also has forgiven you. Ephesians 4:26-32.*

Anger in Its Relationship to One's Self. Ephesians 4:26-27,31

A DESCRIPTION OF PERMISSIVE ANGER

Anger is commanded

Paul wrote, *"Be angry, and yet do not sin."* *"Angry"* as used in this verse is *orgidzesthe*, a word used to describe God's wrath. It is a more settled or abiding condition of the mind. Amazingly, anger here is a present imperative. The Lord is commanding a believer to be angry. However, the word gives a clarification *"and yet do not sin."* This could be categorized as anger exercising a righteous indignation. Jesus revealed a righteous anger when He drove the moneychangers out of the temple. A believer may see a mother who is verbally and physically abusing a child and immediately become angry. When anger is aroused in an observer, is this anger a sin? The answer is no, unless it does not subside and grows into resentment.

If a Christian views evil acts and does not feel a righteous anger, they are not in fellowship with the Holy Spirit. Paul, under the leadership of the Holy Spirit commanded the believer to be angry. It grieves the Holy Spirit for believers to see evil acted out and enjoy it. Paul expressed this righteous anger while in Philippi. A slave girl was following him, *"having a spirit of divination...who was bringing her masters much profit by fortune telling. Following after Paul and us, she kept crying out, saying, 'these men are bondservants of the Most High God, who are proclaiming to you the way of salvation. And she continued doing this for many days. But Paul was greatly annoyed, and turned and said to the spirit, 'I command you in the name of Jesus Christ to come out of her!' And it came out at that very moment."* Acts 16:16-18.

Anger is to be controlled

The admonition is, *"and sin not."* *"Sin"* is *amartano*, which means missing the mark. This word is also a present imperative. This command is as important as the proceeding one, if not more. God designed man after His own emotional nature. The command is to refrain from sin. Anger expressed as an emotion, should not control your actions and attitudes. The Lord never gives a command, which is impossible to follow. These two commands can be followed; which means Christians are without excuse. The Bible is filled with passages illustrating sinful anger. Note what God proclaimed in Proverbs 29:22, *"An angry man stirs up strife, and a hot-tempered man abounds in transgressions."* Anger can develop into sin as rapidly as any emotion. Anger becomes sin, when its reason for existing goes counter to God's nature and person. If God's response would be love and forgiveness and man's response is unforgiveness, then anger has developed into sin.

This passage also teaches anger is a choice. *"...and yet do not sin."* God does not give a command that is impossible for a believer to obey. If anger could not be controlled, then God through Paul gave an impossible command. Anger is a choice of the mind. One can choose to be angry or choose not to be angry. If someone states, "I cannot control my anger!" It reveals one of three things. They have chosen not to allow the Spirit of God to control them. They have a stronghold on the level of the flesh and it needs to be destroyed. The last option is they are not saved. When an irritation comes, a believer has the option of submitting the irritation to the Lord. Since anger is a choice of the mind, all that is needed is a strong deterrent.

Let's assume someone shoves a believer with a temper problem and anger immediately surfaces. As the man turns to see who did the shoving, an immediate damper is placed on his anger when a 6' 9", 300 pound, muscular athlete is the shover. Anger drains from his face, and a sickly smile appears. This illustrates anger can be controlled. In this case another emotion, fear, controlled the believer. Any believer desiring to control his or her anger should find a deterrent that through practice will keep a lid on the boiling pot of anger. He may decide to crawl down the aisle of the church and make an open confession regarding the details of his sin each time he fails to control it. One of the best deterrents for anger is love, which has forgiveness as its expression.

Anger is not to be corrupted

Paul admonished the believers in Ephesus to not let the sun "*go down on your anger.*" "*Anger*" is a different word in the Greek than the word wrath. The Greek word is *parorgismos*. This word points to the irritation, which provoked the anger. This word means anger, an angry mood, a violent irritation, which may be revealed by hiding oneself from others, by flaming looks, harmful words or inconsiderate actions. If a person hits his finger with a hammer, anger is aroused, but subsides, since the hammer is an impersonal object. However, if some other person hits the finger with a hammer, anger could be stored up for years. Paul has indicated that anger arising out of the emotions should be short lived. If a day passes and anger is still in existence, the believer has sinned. Paul admonishes believers to keep anger from ripening into resentment or bitterness. He wrote, "*Do not let the sun go down...*" Not only does it indicate Christians can control anger but it should be controlled the day it flares up.

A DESCRIPTION OF PROVOCATIVE ANGER

Internalized anger

Since Paul describes the various expressions of anger, I will jump ahead and examine these so that anger can be seen in some of its ramifications. Three of these descriptive terms are internalized and affect one's attitudes and actions. The other two describe anger as expressed outwardly to others. "*Let all bitterness and wrath and anger and clamor be put away from you, along with all malice.*" Ephesians 4:31.

The definition of *bitterness* is to cut, to prick, hence pointed, sharp, keen. It is used here as bitter hatred. Bitterness is a state of mind, which keeps a person in a continuous state of animosity. It will make that person harsh, unloving, mean and often repulsive. It is an alienating element of personality and is often projected by a negative attitude. The writer of Hebrews states, "*See to it no one comes short of the grace of God, that no root of bitterness springing up causes trouble, and by it many be defiled.*" Hebrews 12:15. The key words are "*come short of the grace of God.*" Remember grace is unmerited favor. Paul expressed this when he wrote, "*Let no unwholesome word proceed from your mouth, but only such a word as is good for edification according to the need of the moment, that it may give grace to those who hear."* Ephesians 4:29. Paul did not say to those who deserve a good word but to those who have a need. This means believers are to be grace givers. God's grace demands that those who receive His grace, give it to others.

The next word is *wrath*. The Greek word for *wrath* is *orge*. Orge is a type of anger, which is slow in being aroused, but is more lasting in nature. It is a deep flowing anger. This type of anger will hold grudges or take revenge. James used *orge* in his warning to believers, *"But let everyone be quick to hear, slow to speak and slow to anger; for the anger of man does not achieve the righteousness of God."* James 1:19-20. Only God has a right to express wrath. When a Christian allows wrath to control his life, he assumes the right of God's judgement. Prolonged wrath, which is revealed in resentment or bitterness, is a judgmental decision, about the life and worth of another person. Samson is an example of wrath. Notice how he prayed, *"O Lord God, please remember me and please strengthen me just this time, O God, that I may at once be avenged of the Philistines for my two eyes."* Judges 16:28.

Anger in the Greek is *thumos*. Thumos is a type of anger, which reveals a more agitated state of the emotions. It is usually seen in sudden outbursts. It is being hot tempered. Often thumos settles into a prolonged anger, orge - wrath. It is seen in those people who enjoy giving others a piece of their mind. One should be extremely careful in manifesting their anger toward others, including God. Many times thumos will subside as quickly as it arises. This could be called impulsive anger. This type of anger directed toward a person could be sin. However, if it is directed toward a performance, an act or an attitude it is probable, righteous indignation.

Interpersonal anger

Two words are used to describe interpersonal anger. *"Clamor"* is *krauge* in the Greek. Krauge was the sound of the crow's call, as imitated by man. It denotes an outcry. This is the cry of strife. It is the clamor of strife and controversy. This comes as a result of anger. Clamor can describe a lynch mob or an attitude similar to those who clamored for Christ's crucifixion. The people in an uproar said, *"Away with this man, and release for us Barabbas! ...And Pilate, wanting to release Jesus, addressed them again, but they kept on calling out, saying, 'Crucify, crucify Him!'"* There is no room in a believer's life for this outward expression of anger. There is no place in the Bible where this is encouraged.

"*Slander*" in the Greek is *blasphemia*. It is a combination of *blapto*, to injure and *pheme*, speech. It is speaking evil of someone. It is a more enduring manifestation of inward anger that reveals itself in reviling. This may be motivated by other emotions such as jealousy. Paul uses this word in writing to Timothy, "*...but he has a morbid interest in controversial questions and disputes about words, out of which arise envy strife, abusive language, evil suspicions.*" 1 Timonthy 6:4. The Pharisees accused Jesus of casting out demons by the power of Beelzebulb the ruler of the demons. Luke 11:15. Slander as an outward expression of anger and has no place in a believer's life. This is anger expressed as sin. It must be rejected and confessed if committed.

DANGERS IN PROLONGED ANGER

Anger prevents an attitude of submission

Paul wrote, "*...and do not give the devil an opportunity.*" "*Give*" is a present imperative. It is a definite command with the continuing results of not giving an opportunity to the devil. Failure to control ones anger is violating a commandment of the Lord. Submission to God is the basis for a Christ-controlled life. In order to repulse Satan, a believer must submit to God's commands. James states, "*Submit, therefore, to God, resist the devil and he will flee from you.*" James 4:7. If a believer fails to submit, then the devil does not have to flee and can continue to harass the believer. Peter wrote, "*Be of sober spirit, be on the alert. Your adversary, the devil, prowls about like a roaring lion, seeking someone to devour.*" 1 Peter 5:8. To be of sober spirit is to be in control of self, not under the control of a fleshly emotion. Often believers think they are immune from Satan's attack, because they attend church. This is far from the truth. The only requirement set forth by God is submission. When he wrote, "*Be on the alert. Your adversary, the devil, prowls about like a roaring lion, seeking someone to devour,*" Peter was warning Christians of the devil's destructive power. When a believer knowingly is angry over a prolonged period of time, he is in rebellion against God. This is a deliberate violation of God's will. Actually he is assuming the rights of God. Paul wrote, "*Never pay back evil for evil to anyone. Respect what is right in the sight of all men. If possible, so far as it depends on you, be at peace with all men. Never take your own revenge, but leave room for the wrath of God, for it is written, 'Vengeance is Mine, I will repay,' says* the Lord." Romans 12:17-19. Therefore when believers are angry over a period of time they are not in submission to God. To be in submission anger and resentment must be confessed and released.

Anger permits an attack by Satan

Paul also wrote, *"And do not give the devil an opportunity."* *"Opportunity"* is *topos*, which means a place, location or opportunity. The word topography is a derivative of this word. It was used in describing a region or a locality. Paul was indicating that a believer gives the devil an opportunity (ground) to wage war against him or her, because they have allowed anger to control their actions instead of the Holy Spirit. Prolonged anger violates a spiritual law, which permits this attack. In most cases the devil wages war on believers on the soul level. The soul is the mind, will, and emotions. The emotions and mind can come under Satan's oppressive power when anger is allowed to control the believer. Anger provides the forces of evil ground to wage war against the saints. Anger removes the armor of God and provides the enemy's fiery darts an available target. One of his fiery darts is leading Christians to believe they are immune to his attacks, since they are followers of the Lord. This is contrary to the Word.

Anger in Its Relationship to Other Saints

A DEMAND FOR WORKS OF GRACE

Paul admonishes the believer by writing, *"Let no unwholesome word proceed from your mouth."* In the Greek *"unwholesome"* is *sapros*, which means corrupt, rank, foul, putrid, and rotten. When anger controls your temper things are said, which cannot be taken back. James gives an apt description of the tongue. *"The tongue is afire, the very world of iniquity; the tongue is set among our members as that which defiles the entire body, and sets on fire the course of our life, and is set on fire by hell... It is a restless evil and full of deadly poison."* James 3:6-8. James indicates the forces of evil use the tongue. This has to be the meaning of *"and is set on fire by hell."* In this passage Paul uses the word "proceed." Proceed is a present imperative. Let no unwholesome word proceed from the mouth is not an impossible command. The tongue can and must be controlled. Jesus said, *"...and whoever **shall say** you fool, shall be guilty enough to go into the fiery hell."* Matthew 5:22. Paul made this same appeal to the Colossians. *"Let your speech always be with grace, seasoned, as it were, with salt, so that you may know how to respond to each person."* Colossians 4:6. The use of salt is not only to flavor one's speech, but to preserve it. This passage does not condone salty language.

This passage is also a prohibition about uncontrolled anger *"Proceed from your mouth."* In the Greek *"proceed"* is a present imperative. It has the meaning of going out or coming out. This is the Lord's command to control your tongue. Proverbs 16:32 relates the blessing in the control of your anger. *"He who is slow to anger is better than the mighty, and he who rules his spirit than he who captures a city."* Other scriptures relating to controlling one's temper are, *"A fool always loses his temper, but a wise man holds it back."* Proverbs 29:11. *"An angry man stirs up strife and a hot tempered man abounds in transgressions."* Proverbs 29:22. *"A man of great anger shall bear the penalty, for if you rescue him, you will only have to do it again."* Proverbs 19:19.

A DEMAND FOR WORDS OF GRACE

Paul wrote, *"...but only such a word as is good for edification according to the need of the moment that it may give grace to those who hear."* This statement by Paul runs counter to the natural bent of man. The normal reaction is to praise those who deserve it. Paul wrote to praise those who need it even if they don't deserve it. Paul uses the word *"edification."* In the Greek *"edification"* is *oikodeme,* a combination of oikos, house and demo, to build. This is the act of erecting a building, used in a spiritual sense of promoting or building spiritual growth. Believers are to use words, which build character and enhance spiritual development.

Edification requires love, joy, peace, patience, understanding, kindness, or in short, all the fruit of the Spirit. Paul is appealing to the motive of the believer. It is to build up, not tear down. It is to act like Christ. We would be devastated if God did not give believers grace to make mistakes. Parents can destroy their children through critical words rather than godly words of praise. This may have been in Paul's mind when he wrote to the church at Rome, "So then let us pursue the things which make for peace and the **building up** (edification) of one another."

Christians are to be alert to a grace need. Paul wrote, *"According to the need of the moment."* Need is simply to have need of something. This passage could be translated, "the building up of the need," or "to supply that which is needed." The need represents a weakness in someone's life, which the word "edify" or "build up" encourages the believer to assist in strengthening. Sinful anger is often rooted in self-centeredness, which ignores the needs of others. Anger blinds believers to the deep needs of others. Edification or building up of others causes a believer to see others as opportunities to minister. The natural tendency is to look at a problem as it affects your self instead of viewing it as opportunity to bring God into the situation.

Christians are commanded to give out grace, *"...that it may give grace to those who hear."* In the Greek *"grace"* is *charis*, which means unmerited favor. It is bestowing from a loving disposition, kindness, goodness, mercy and graciousness. From God's perspective, man does not deserve or earn His love, mercy and salvation. God gives to man grace out of His loving nature to undeserving sinners. Christians are saved by grace and should live by grace. **Grace is defined as unmerited favor.** Christians receive eternal life through grace not by good works. Therefore believers are to be **grace givers**. Practically, this is giving an encouraging word when someone deserves much less. It is speaking forth words which build up and not tear down. Christians often say "I will compliment them when they deserve it." Grace words build an individual up when it is not deserved. Note that edification using grace is given to all who hear, including bystanders. Spiritual maturity is caught as much as taught, from those who are spiritually mature. The scripture states, *"A gentle answer turns away wrath, but a harsh word stirs up anger."* Proverbs 15:1. God gives grace to the believer so that he can give grace by encouraging and building up those who don't deserve it.

Anger in Its Relationship with the Holy Spirit

A REACTION TO DISOBEDIENCE

The nature of the command

Paul wrote, "*And do not grieve the Holy Spirit.*" The Greek word for "*grieve*" is lupeo, which means to cause sorrow, to grieve. Grieve is a present imperative, a command to cease grieving the Holy Spirit. Since it is in the present tense, it forbids the habitual and continuous acts of sin. Words, which tear down other believers, grieve the Holy Spirit. These words would be in direct opposition of the Holy Spirit's work, which is to build up. Can you picture the Father weeping each time a Christian speaks contemptuous words to another believer? Outwardly expressed anger is seldom directed toward the Holy Spirit. However, in directing it toward others, it is directed toward the Holy Spirit who indwells believers. This short statement should be etched in the mind and heart of all Christians and motivate them to not sin against the Lord. The immediate response might be, "I didn't sin against God, because I was angry with a brother." John wrote, "*The one who says he is in the light and yet hates his brother is in the darkness until now. The one who loves his brother abides in the light and there is no cause for stumbling in him. But the one who hates his brother is in the darkness and walks in the darkness, and does not know where he is going because the darkness has blinded his eyes.*" 1 John 2:9-11.

The nature of His grief

It is essential to look at the nature of the Holy Spirit's grief. Sin offends the Holy Spirit's nature. When believers offend one another, the God of love is grieved because of the absence of love, mercy and grace. Sins, which deter spiritual growth adversely, affect the work of the Holy Spirit. Jesus said, "*And I will ask the Father, and He will give you another Helper, that He may be with you forever; that is the Spirit of truth, whom the world cannot receive, because it does not behold Him or know Him.*" Other passages indicate the Holy Spirit is to guide into all truth, illuminate the words of Jesus, impart power, infill the believer, and bring forth fruit. When anger controls the believer, the Holy Spirit's work is shelved. A believer may exhort another believer regarding certain standards and when his counsel is ignored, the believer is grieved knowing that the individual is missing God's best. A believer may grieve because the consequence of another's actions often brings needless suffering and pain. This is a small picture of how the Holy Spirit grieves. The Holy Spirit grieves when believers live according to the flesh and not under His power. He knows they are missing God's best. The deeds of the flesh are destructive to the believer's walk. **Paul has stressed the greatest motivation for controlling anger, do not grieve the Holy Spirit.**

A REASON FOR OBEDIENCE

The principle of being sealed

Paul gives a spiritual reason for controlling anger. In this passage he wrote, "*...whom you were sealed for the day of redemption.*" In the Greek the term "*sealed*" signified, a finished transaction, ownership and security. It is an aorist passive which reveals a completed act in past time. A believer is already sealed for the day of redemption. The sealing is not future but past. This gives believers an assurance of salvation. However, this does not give the believer the freedom to allow sin to reign in his life. Since believers have this hope it should motivate them in their attitude toward others. This is an assurance so that the enemy cannot destroy a believer's hope. Because of this hope it should motivate Christians to work at salvation as if everything depended on them and to trust in the Lord as if everything depended on Him.

The purpose of being sealed

Needless to say, everything does depend on God. This sealing took place when the believer was born again. It has an eternal guarantee. The sealing is present but also future. Paul wrote, "*...For the day of redemption.*" "*Redemption*" is a combination of *apo*, from and *lutrosis*, a redemption. It is literally, a releasing payment of a ransom. It is forgiveness, justification, and redemption as a result of your sins being covered. The redeemed one has been delivered from the guilt and punishment of his sins. The redemption of a believer's sins comes through the Lord Jesus Christ.

This is described in Ephesians 1:7, *"In Him we have redemption through His blood, the forgiveness of our trespasses, according to the riches of His grace."* The final act of redemption is the deliverance of believers from the presence and power of sin at the coming of the Lord Jesus Christ. Because of this present and future forgiveness, Christians should act as god-fearing men and women. The controlling desire should be to please Him and not self.

Real Life Illustration

An adult male believer had a tremendous anger problem. He would blow his cool even in public. He justified this anger by saying "This is just the way I am. I can't help it." He seemed to think that he was born with his anger and therefore his anger was not controllable. He was angry with his family, friends and neighbors. People walked as if on eggshells around him. Actually no one felt he could be a real friend for fear of his anger. By failing to control his weakness he lost out on the joy, which comes from being with friends. If anger can be controlled in church at eleven on Sunday morning, it can be controlled anytime. Unfortunately this believer never learned the truth of controlling his anger, since he did not accept the fact it could be controlled.

Verbal Commitment to the Lord

I confess that I have allowed anger to remain overnight. I know that this is sin. I readily acknowledge the flesh is active and alive and warring against the Spirit. I choose to learn to control the emotion of anger. I will determine to develop a personal but costly way to deter it from controlling my life. I know that a strong deterrent will assist in this control. I will dedicate myself to becoming a grace giver. I am reminded that a soft word turns away wrath. I realize anger originates as a result of pride. Since pride got Satan kicked out of heaven, he enjoys playing on it like harp strings in believer's lives. The sin of anger and pride causes a breech in fellowship with the Father. I desire fellowship not alienation.

Thought Provoking Questions

1. What ticks you off the quickest? Do you get angry when you don't get your way? Do you get angry when someone lets you down?

2. Is anger the result of wounded pride? If so, should it be?

3. When righteous anger is justified, does it include a critical attitude, harshness, unkindness, irritability or crankiness?

4. What determines the cause of anger?

5. What are some deterrents that will assist the believer in controlling anger?

† Warfare Prayer

Father, I confess the sin of anger. I know that it arises from pride. I recognize that anger is an emotional reaction acquired and developed over the years. I am willing to confess each and every time I was angry and sin was the result. Any past expression of anger that influences my life today, needs to be removed. I ask the Holy Spirit to reveal it to me so it can be confessed. I ask that the power behind these past experiences of anger be broken and will no longer have the ability to influence me. I ask forgiveness for grieving the Holy Spirit. I know that allowing anger to control my actions and attitude is to walk under the influence of the flesh. I ask you to bring to my attention a deterrent that will remind me to control anger. I do not wish to give the wicked one an opportunity to attack me or anyone I am associated with.

STEPS OF ACTION

• Accept the fact that anger is controllable by stating aloud, "I have an anger problem, but I will with God's help bring it under control."

• Analyze your anger problem by reflecting upon your past history of anger. Ask yourself, what has caused my anger to rage out of control? What ticks me off the quickest? When was the first time I really got angry? Write down the answers and reflect on them, asking God to reveal the root cause if it is not evident. If the root cause is revealed or known, confess it to the Lord.

• Remember believers are dead to the power of anger, but not to the emotion of anger. God can deliver from any stronghold including anger. Begin confessing that God has given you power to overcome through His Spirit

• Find a deterrent, when practiced, which will tend to prevent anger. Remember anger is a choice of the mind. You can choose not to be angry, even when your soul man is crying our for revenge.

• When anger is uncontrollable, it has become a stronghold. Session 12 will deal with the tearing down of a stronghold with steps of action.

Chapter 7

❧

A Parable on Uncontrolled Emotions
Luke 15:25-32

The following are a few questions which need to be answered before a believerbegins this study. Be honest and answer each question without supposing what God would have you write.

1. Having studied the first 6 chapters, do you feel you have conquered most of your emotional liabilities?

2. Suppose you owned a calf and you had a wayward brother come to your house, after living a immoral life, and your family killed the calf and threw a party even hiring a band and you were ignored and not invited to the party, what would be your reaction?

3. How much sin can a person commit which will not be covered by love and grace?

4. Do you have a relative or acquaintance whose life-style is atrocious? If this person confessed his sin how would you receive him? Would it be with open arms of love or would you have a wait and see attitude?

Introduction

This parable illustrates many of the truths already taught in the first few chapters. It is apparent the older brother had a lack of love and compassion. The first half of the parable which is all about the younger brother is usually what is preached from the pulpit. However, the parable was to illustrate the attitude of the father and younger son compared to the older brother.

The second half of this parable, which is commonly called the parable of the prodigal son, illustrates the attitude of the Pharisees toward sinners. It also describes the attitude of anyone and especially believers, who allow their emotions to control them. This older brother reveals the following emotions, depression, anger, resentment, jealousy, rejection and hate. True forgiveness would have eliminated the control of these emotions. A parable is a story illustrating a truth or truths. This parable has more than one truth. The older brother felt shame and embarrassment because of his brother's sins. This man's reaction to his younger brother and to his father reveals the sin of pride. Pride is the root or cause of many excessive emotions. In this parable the older brother resents the younger brother and even resents the father for forgiving and welcoming him home. Pride and self-righteousness made him think of himself as so worthy and the younger brother as so unworthy. This parable was directed to the self-righteous religious leaders, who looked down their noses at those they called sinners. A question needs to be answered, of the two sons, who was the greatest sinner?

> **Text:** *"Now his older son was in the field, and when he came and approached the house, he heard music and dancing. And he summoned one of the servants and began inquiring what these things might be. And he said to him, 'Your brother has come, and your father has killed the fattened calf, because he has received him back safe and sound.' But he became angry, and was not willing to go in; and his father came out and began entreating him. But he answered and said to his father, 'Look! For so many years I have been serving you, and I have never neglected a command of yours; and yet you have never given me a kid that I might be merry with my friends; but when this son of yours came, who has devoured your wealth with harlots, you killed the fattened calf for him.' And he said to him, 'My child, you have always been with me, and all that is mine is yours., but we had to be merry and rejoice, for this brother of yours was dead and has begun to live, and was lost and has been found.'" Luke 15:25-32.*

A Disposition of the Older Brother's Emotions

HE FELT REJECTED

The parable indicates he was unaware of the party. *"Now his older son was in the field, and when he came and approached the house, he heard music and dancing."* *"Music"* in the Greek is a word which indicates a band of players or singers. The father had hired a band, and invited the younger brother's friends, killed and cooked a fattened calf, yet had not sent word to the older son. The older brother knew to invite a band and send invitations to friends would take considerable time. Preparations had to be made which took considerable time. Remember the phone had not been invented. The younger brother had been home, for a few days, and the older brother was not informed. He felt an immediate rejection. Everyone at some time has been excluded from some special occasion and felt a degree of rejection. The older brother revealed an angry attitude, since he asked the servant what was going on, instead of going into the house and finding out. This also indicated a suspicious nature. He was expecting to be rejected.

HE EXPRESSED ANGER AND RESENTMENT

"But he became angry, and was not willing to go in; and his father came out and began entreating him." Apparently word had spread among those attending the party that the older son had arrived and was hot under the collar. This older son wanted everyone to know of his disapproval, anger and resentment. Resentment and anger motivates isolation from others, including friends and loved ones. Often the thinking or motivation of rejection is, "I will hurt them by not showing my face." Anger and resentment, left unchecked, leads to bitterness. The anger and resentment against the younger brother did not begin with not being invited to the party. The older brother had been angry and resentful for a long time.

HIS EXPRESSED THE FEELING OF NEGLECT

It is difficult to believe a loving father would have neglected his older son. He said, *"Look! For so many years I have been serving you, and I have never neglected a command of yours; and yet you have never given me a kid, that I might be merry with my friends."* The older son revealed a resentment of the father for neglecting to throw him a party. Remember the inheritance was divided among the sons. He had the resources to have a party anytime he wished. A feeling of neglect usually indicates an expression of self pity. He indicated his obedience and faithfulness for years as a reason for feeling neglected. Everyone at some time has felt or experienced the feeling of neglect. This type of feeling is a part of the old flesh and is stirred up by the sin of pride.

Deception Brought About by His Emotions

HE WAS DECEIVED ABOUT HIS VIRTUE

He said, *"I have never neglected a command of yours."* He knew the father's will regarding the younger son, or there would not have been instant anger. He knew the father's forgiving nature. The older son and father were aware of the immoral practices of the younger brother. It had caused shame and embarrassment for the family name. As a result, he rebelled against his father's will and loving nature and refused to make peace with his brother. His declaration of right living was clouded by his emotions. He was not nearly as virtuous as he thought. In verse 28 the father went out and "... *began entreating him."* *"Entreating"* is in the perfect tense and indicates the father was pleading over and over for the older son to relent. This irate man was breaking his father's heart, disobeying his father's desires, while verbally maintaining his loyalty and fidelity to the father's will. He was a picture of the self-righteous Pharisees. This picture is typical of those who point their fingers at others.

HE WAS DECEIVED ABOUT REAL VALUES

He said, *"You have never given me a kid, that I might be merry with my friends."* The implication in this statement was "You have never taken a less expensive baby goat and thrown me a party, much less kill a fattened calf " This type of response indicates that doing things for me is more important than being a loving father who had given him his inheritance. The father responded by saying, *"all that is mine is yours."* The older brother had everything. He was selfish and self-centered and did not wish for the father to show his love to anyone else. When anger, resentment and pride prevail, usually a comparison is made about tangible items, overlooking the benefits of love. Resentment carries the idea others have received more than me.

HIS DECEPTION BLURRED HIS VISION

"But when this son of yours came, who had devoured his living with harlots." He used the words *"son of yours,"* instead of this brother of mine. Excessive emotion had blinded him to his brother's character. He was unconcerned that his brother was repentant. The younger son had confessed to the father as related by Jesus in 15:21. If the older son had asked, "Did he repent of his misdeeds?" It would have shown he had compassion. There was no concern about the younger brother's repentance. The father did not mention it to the older son, perhaps he thought it would not do any good. The older brother was also blind to his brother's needs. He needed love and forgiveness. He had a need for friends who were more than fair weather friends. He came to himself while dying with hunger. He was willing to become a hired servant to the father. Since the inheritance was divided, all the father's possessions belonged to the older brother. Can you imagine being a servant to the older brother?

Defiance Brought About Because of His Emotions

The father was the head of the home according to their custom. The older brother has observed this authority while the younger brother had rebelled. The father had the **authority and right** to receive and restore the son. He did not give the younger son the older brother's estate, only love and forgiveness. The older son resisted the father's right to forgive by refusing to forgive. When a Christian imitates the older son and will not forgive, he attacks the purpose of forgiveness and the heavenly Father's right to forgive. Remember this parable is a picture of the Father and His children, believers. Forgiveness is freeing the offender from any punishment for his offenses. All offenses are against God, and if He forgives others of their sins, it behooves the believer to also forgive.

The older brother also defied the **father's reason** for forgiving. The basic reason for forgiveness is grace. Grace is unmerited favor. The younger son had not merited forgiveness by earning it. Instead, through love, the father showed grace. The older son's attitude was to let him pay the price for his sin. The Father shows grace to all believers; it is with the desire they also show grace. Since all men are sinners and fall short of God's holy nature, they cannot earn His favor. Therefore, He gives grace. Believers are to become grace givers to other believers. Giving out grace means that a person has not earned the right of forgiveness. However, love mandates forgiveness, and so forgiveness is given to an offender even though it is undeserved.

Destructiveness Brought About by Emotions

It Caused a Division in the Family's Fellowship

Uncontrolled emotions like anger and resentment cause a division in fellowship. In the parable, Luke writes, *"... and his father came out."*

As has been noted, a servant reported to the father the older son's emotional state. Word probably circulated among the party goers that the older brother was upset. By refusing to join the festivities, he communicated his anger and resentment outwardly toward his younger brother, his father and even the invited guests. Excessive emotions out of control cause a breach in fellowship. The fellowship between the brothers was broken and was in danger between the father and older son. When someone is self-centered, angry and resentful, they usually do not care what others think or feel. They are so wrapped up in self that they cannot see the destructiveness of their actions. Churches have split, families have lost fellowship with one another because of resentment and anger and the unwillingness to forgive.

IT CAUSED A DAMPER ON THE FAMILY'S FESTIVITY

Uncontrolled emotions as seen as seen in this parable clamp a damper on festivity. When the father left the party to reconcile his older son, a buzz must have gone through the guests. Something must be terribly wrong for the host to leave. The host leaving a party was rare. Surely a report was made known about the feelings of the older son. Some may have questioned if the party would continue. Would the older brother run off the younger? Would there be a fight? What would be the outcome? The joy of the occasion was dampened by the attitude of the older brother. This is also true in a church or home celebration. In a church setting, guests can sense a charged atmosphere when there is emotional conflict. How can a church have a praise attitude when members of the church family are visibly showing their resentment for other members? How can a family have a festive occasion when resentment is evident? It is like walking on eggshells so to speak.

IT DESTROYED USEFULNESS
IN THE FAMILY RELATIONSHIPS

Uncontrolled emotions destroy usefulness in families and church families. Anger and resentment reveal and openly display an attitude of distrust. This is what is seen in the older sons attitude. His did not trust his father's decision to forgive. As a result the family circle had been broken. The older son could not participate in any of the festivities because of his attitude. Friends and the community saw the unity of the family as fragile if not broken. When this happens in a family or church it will hinder their effectiveness and influence over others. Distrust was underlying the remarks of the older son. He said, "*...but when this son of yours came, who has devoured your wealth with harlots, you killed the fattened calf for him.*" The older brother did not say the younger brother's wealth, but your wealth. He probably had a problem with the younger son before he left home. He may have these thoughts, "Why are you doing this?" "Are you going to give him part of my inheritance?" The older brother, knowing the father's compassion, was fearful about what would come next. Excessive emotions promote the attitude of distrust among family and church members.

It Caused a Display of Disrespect

Emotions like those of the older brother display an attitude of disrespect. He said, *"Look! For so many years..."* instead of saying, "Father, for so many years." He did not use an endearing term of respect for the father, but revealed he was on a high horse of anger. Also in this verse he said, "I have been serving you." The word serve is used to serve as a servant. He indicates that he was serving as a hired servant not as a son. He was saying you have bossed me around all these years and have done nothing for me. He must have thought, "You are treating this rascal like royalty, and you have been treating me like dirt." Anger between spouses often reveals attitudes of disrespect, which in turn create a breach in relationships. Anger and resentment is nothing more than pride exploiting itself to the determent of others. Humility shows a respect for others and a submission to God; whereas resentment reveals the opposite, a total disrespect for others and especially those in authority.

Emotions as showed in the older brother **display an attitude of displeasure**. The older brother wanted his father, brother, servants and friends to know he was not pleased. Emotions cry out to be heard. Normally unless they are revealed to others, they cannot be nurtured. **The older brother was getting pleasure out of showing his displeasure**. The attitude that is usually communicated is, "I am mad and I do not care who knows it." Anger, after it is expressed grants a certain satisfaction physically and emotionally. It feeds the ego and makes the person feel justified. If expressing emotional feelings brought about instant pain instead of pleasure, the attitude of displeasure would disappear. The forces of evil laugh in glee when Christians display displeasure in the same manner as the older brother displayed. They want you to feel good about exploding. However, remember it grieves the Holy Spirit.

A Decision Brought About by the Father's Attitude

THE FATHER ADMONISHES THE SON

The father admonished his son **regarding his attitude.** He said, *"My child, you have always been with me."* The Greek for *"child"* is *teknon.* Teknon gives prominence to the fact of birth while the other Greek word for son, *"huios,"* stresses the dignity and character of the relationship. Jesus in telling this parable used teknon which is a tender, affectionate term. He did not use huios, which would have stressed character. Jesus pictured the son as acting out of character as a son and more like a child. Emotions out of control make believers act childish. One of the sayings for people on their high horse is "Quit acting like a baby." The father wanted the son to straighten up and fly right. This picture should encourage believers since it is a picture of how God relates to His children. The father admonished his son in **regard to acceptance.** The father said, "For this brother of yours." He did not say, this son of mine. The father pointed out the relationship between the two. Anger in a family elicits this type of response of the older brother. "This son of yours," role has been replayed millions of times as one person blames another, or refuses to take responsibility. Jesus depicted the father as desiring the older brother to accept his brother with feelings and compassion. As has been shown, the older brother should have said, "If I had the choice of choosing any brother in the world, I would choose him. If I had the authority to change him, I would not change him in any way I would leave him as God has created him. For God does have that power and it is His problem. I thank God he is my brother."

THE FATHER'S APPEAL TO THE SON

The father also appealed to the son on the basis of a **permanent relationship**. *"My child, you have always been with me."* The father was saying, since we have this continuous relationship with one another, why should it bother you that I reestablish a relationship with my other son? He could have said, "Stop showing your green eyed jealousy about my love for your brother. This will not hinder our relationship." The father knew the son had always been with him as a son not a slave. By using *teknon*, he revealed the birth and right of the older son. This is also a picture of a believer's relationship with the Father. If God desires to grant blessings to others why should believers show jealousy? Christians are children of God and have a permanent relationship with Him. What He does for others should not destroy this relationship.

The appeal reminded his son of his **personal riches**. He said, *"And all that is mine is yours."* The father had divided the estate between the sons as seen in 15:12, "...and the younger of them said to his father, *'Father give me the share of the estate that falls to me.'* And he divided his wealth between them." Everything belonging to the father belonged to the older son. He could not give him anymore since he had it all. It seems the older brother wanted all of his love as well. Believers have been adopted as sons. They are heirs, joint heirs with Christ. There should be no resentment toward others or God in His bestowal of love, forgiveness or grace. When a son has everything, he does not need anything else. Believers have been adopted as sons and have the blessings of being children of God.

The appeal reminded the son of the **purpose of rejoicing**. The father said, *"But we had to be merry and rejoice, for this brother of yours was dead and has begun to live, and was lost and has been found."* The rejoicing was the result of repentance. In Luke 15:10 Jesus said, *"In the same way, I tell you, there is joy in the presence of the angels of God over one sinner who repents."* The three parables in this chapter reveal how people rejoice. The first two parables are over things of which there is little value. The last parable is over a brother who is a divine creation. In the eyes of God all repentant sinners are extremely valuable. God loved us so much He died on the cross. The younger brother had repented of his sins. This mandated forgiveness and joy.

Restoration is the result of repentance. The father said, *"This brother of yours was dead and has begun to live and was lost and has been found."* The nature of repentance is bringing a person to become more like God. Angels rejoice over the character of God. Why not over men who exemplify a part of that character, by turning from a life of edifying the flesh and Satan, to God. If one rejoices over finding animals or money as depicted in the first two parables in this chapter, then how much more over a lost brother or son? The nature of parental love has forgiveness as its base. The love of God demands grace and forgiveness be shown. The older brother displayed a judgmental attitude toward the younger brother. Jesus said, *"And do not judge and you will not be judged; and do not condemn, and you will not be condemned; pardon and you will be pardoned."* Luke 6:36. Did the older brother reconcile with the younger brother? Why didn't Jesus finish the story and tell the outcome? Perhaps everyone who reads or hears the parable has the potential of finishing the story in his or her life. Take a moment and reflect about God's love and forgiveness. Is there anyone you need to forgive? Why not do it now.

Real Life Illustration

A lady I counseled with three times depicted the attitudes of the older brother. She had resentment for a family member. She could not forgive. She would say, "You do not understand how bad I was hurt and you are asking me to forgive. I would never have him in my home. I don't believe God wants me to forgive him." This woman allowed her resentment to make her bitter. No one wanted to be her friend because this resentment could not be reserved for the family member alone. It spread into every area of her life. The last report I had she was still in therapy. As far as I know she never changed. This was tragic, because she refused to forgive; she invited the torturers to attack her emotional life. She could not believe what Jesus said in Matthew 18:21-35.

Verbal Commitment to the Lord

I confess at times I have felt or acted like the older brother. I know I must not be judgmental. For the manner in which I judge I will be judged. I choose to forgive others no matter what they have done, I recognize grace is giving others the same love, mercy and compassion which I receive from the Lord. I will not allow anger or resentment to destroy my earthly family or my church family. I pledge to the Lord, I will become a grace giver to others. I choose to complete this story by restoring relationships with those who I have alienated.

Thought Provoking Questions

1. In what way does anger and resentment create a climate of distrust, disrespect and disunity within a body?

2. How do excessive emotions, like the ones in the older brother, cloud logic and permit irrational thinking?

3. Why are excessive emotions, caused by inward feelings of rejections, neglect, and anger, ungodly?

4. Do you have an unfinished story with a parent or brother or know someone who needs to finish the story? What would it take to finish the story?

5. What keeps a Christian from restoring relationships with those who feel alienated? Is it pride and only pride?

† Warfare Prayer

Father, I recognize myself in varying degrees as the older brother. I intend to make peace with you. I do not want to destroy family unity or my own usefulness in your kingdom. I choose to forgive. I know that my emotions may not agree with this choice. I will continue to deny my feelings and exercise faith by forgiving. I know that in time my feelings will coincide with the leadership of Your Spirit. I confess the sin of rebelling against your will by holding resentment for (name). Father, anyone or anything that has occurred in the past which could influence the present, I ask that you set me free from it. I will become a grace giver and participate in rejoicing with those I have forgiven.

STEPS OF ACTION

- Analyze your relations with family, friends, and others, by asking yourself the following questions. Do I feel rejected by anyone? Do I have anger and resentment toward anyone? Do I feel neglected by God and others? Have I created a division of fellowship in my home, church or community? Do I display distrust, disrespect or displeasure toward those who are in authority over me?

- After evaluating yourself, if the answer to some of these questions is yes, then confess those sins to the Lord. After confessing, make things right with the other people. This usually involves personal contact. Can you imagine the older brother saying, "Yes, I do forgive? However, I am not going in to the party, nor do I want to see my younger brother." You might say, "I will forgive but I do not want to fellowship with him." Can you imagine the Father forgiving on that level? He forgives believers of their sin, but He does not want to fellowship with His children? Forgiveness is an act of faith. You may be required to tell your emotions to take a back seat and do what you know is right.

- Remember that you are the older brother and you must take the responsibility for restoring broken relationships. Ask yourself, "As the older brother will I right the relations and make certain the family unity is not broken? Will I make certain the unity of God's family, the church, is also not broken?" Confession of sin requires forgiveness and giving grace to the unloved. Make this decision "I will be a grace giver and will forgive all offences."

- The older brother sinned against the father. When a believer will not forgive those whom God has forgiven, then he has sinned against God. Make certain that you confess the sin of unforgiveness to the heavenly Father.

Chapter 8

❧

The Futility in Anxiety
Matthew 6:25-34

The following are a few questions which need to be answered before a believer begins this study. Be honest and answer each question without supposing what God would have you write.

1. Do you ever have anxiety attacks? If so how often?

2. What is the cause of your anxiety? Is it the lack of money, family relationships etc. List those things, which tend to cause anxiety.

3. Is there a difference between anxiety and worry?

4. In your opinion is worry and anxiety a sin?

5. What does anxiety communicate to God?

Introduction

Anxiety is an emotion. It is worry carried to the extreme. It has been a factor in destroying faith since Adam sinned. Anxiety arises as a result of unbelief. It is a failure to trust God. In the passage we are studying, Jesus told the multitude and the disciples not to be anxious about the future. The future always includes the necessities of life, food, clothing and housing. Undue concern over these and other future or present problems constitutes worry and anxiety. Jesus told the disciples in Matthew 6:30, "*Will He not much more do so for you, O men of little faith?*" In Matthew 6:32, Jesus said, "*...for your heavenly Father knows*

117

that you need all these things." Jesus said that not one sparrow *"...will fall to the ground apart from your Father but the very hairs of your head are all numbered."* Matthew 10:29-30. The fruit of the Spirit, which protects against anxiety, is peace. However, anxiety drives out inner peace. In Philippians 4:6-7, Paul states, *"Be anxious for nothing but in everything by prayer and supplication with thanksgiving let your request be made known to God and the peace of God which surpasses all comprehension, shall guard your hearts and your minds in Christ Jesus."*

> *Text:* "For this reason I say to you, do not be anxious for your life, as to what you shall eat, or what you shall drink; nor for your body, as to what you shall put on. Is not life more than food, and the body clothing? Look at the birds of the air, that they do not sow, neither do they reap, not gather into barns, and yet your heavenly Father feeds them. Are you not worth much more than they? And which of you by being anxious can add a single cubit to his life's span? And why are you anxious about clothing? Observe how the lilies of the field grow, they do not toil nor do they spin, yet I say to you that even Solomon in all his glory did not clothe himself like one of these. But if God so arrays the grass of the field, which is alive today and tomorrow is thrown into the furnace, will He not much more do so for you, O men of little Faith? Do not be anxious then saying, 'What shall we eat?' or 'What shall we drink?' or 'With what shall we clothe ourselves?' For all these things the Gentiles eagerly seek; for your heavenly Father knows that you need all these things. But seek first His kingdom and His righteousness; and all these things shall be added to you. Therefore do not be anxious for tomorrow; for tomorrow will care for itself. Each day has enough trouble of its own." Matthew 6:25-34

The Fallacy in Anxiety

THE CONCERN ABOUT ANXIETY

The definition of anxiety

In this portion of the Sermon on the Mount Jesus commanded the disciples and the multitude not to be anxious. *"For this reason I say to you, do not be anxious for your life... And which of you by being anxious can add a single cubit to his life's span? And why are you anxious about clothing? ... Do not be anxious for tomorrow, for tomorrow will care for itself"* Matthew 6:25,27,28,31,34. This directive of Jesus is applicable for believers of all generations. *"Anxiety"* in the Greek is *merimnao*, which means to draw in different directions, or to distract. Over the years it came to signify that which causes a distraction or that which draws a person in different directions. It came to mean a care, especially an anxious care. *Merimnao* indicates confusion in the mind, a divided mind. Anxiety originates in the mind with thoughts, builds until it consumes one's thinking. This stimulates a variety of emotions such as fear, depression, frustration, anger and often rebellion. Webster states that anxiety is a "painful uneasiness of mind of an impending or anticipated ill." Someone has said, "Worry gives a small thing a big shadow." I heard the following, which stuck in my mind, "Worry is wasting today's time to clutter up tomorrow's opportunities with yesterday's troubles."

The descriptions of anxiety

Anxiety is tomorrow's fears etched into today's emotions. It is a state of being at war with one self and indirectly with God. Anxiety is a futile attempt to control tomorrow, today. It is the negative thoughts of worry projected as real. It is the imagination frantically seeking a solution to an impossible situation. There are varying degrees of anxiety. Anxiety can be seen in most families on a weekly, if not daily basis. There is anxiety over employment, bills, children, a spouse, and the list is endless. The extreme is to allow anxiety to occupy one's emotions until an anxiety attack occurs. A preacher once said, "An average person's anxiety is founded on, 40 % about things which will never happen, 30%

about things in the past which cannot be changed, 12% thinking about criticism by others which is mostly untrue, 10% about health, which gets worse with stress, created by anxiety, and only 8% is about real problems which will be faced."

The distrust in anxiety

Anxiety is concern carried to the extreme. Concern is a natural response of the emotions, which should direct the believer to the Lord. Anxiety is attempting to solve the impossible through the power of the soul. Jesus indicated that trust and faith in God should alleviate your concerns and put to death anxiety. Jesus gave the disciples the assurance of God's sovereignty over all creation. He used birds, lilies and grass to depict this principle. He is not only Creator God, but also Sustainer God. When a believer is preoccupied with anxiety over needs, he is communicating, "God, I can't trust you to meet my needs." This passage in Matthew begins with Jesus saying, *"For this reason I say to you, do not be anxious for your life..."* Matthew 6:25. Immediately the thought comes, "What reason is He talking about?" This passage on anxiety is based on Matthew 6:19-24. Jesus said, *"Do not lay up for yourselves treasures upon earth..."* He concludes by saying, *"No one can serve two masters; for either he will hate the one and love the other; or he will hold to one and despise the other. You cannot serve God and mammon."* Placing your focus on earthly things, shows distrust in the Father's provisions. It is a serving of self by self. It is making self god of one's life. Jesus warned the disciples not to place their focus on earthly things, but the heavenly Father. Anxiety is focusing on earthly things and not on God.

Remember Jesus said you cannot serve two masters. Attempting to serve God and self is in effect committing idolatry. Most Christians who are anxious about their life would argue with this statement. However, when Christians cannot trust the Lord for their everyday needs it indicate they are trusting in themselves. At the end of the discourse Jesus said, *"But seek first His kingdom and His righteousness; and all these things shall be added to you."* Matthew 6:33.

THE CAUSES OF ANXIETY

Unresolved conflicts

Unresolved conflicts are disagreements, anger, or wrongs, which have occurred in the past. They remain unforgiven and are compounded in the mind. These unresolved conflicts create emotional reactions. These emotional reactions sometimes result in a backlash of feelings. Anxiety is one of these emotional expressions. Anxiety brought about because of conflict can dominate a person so much that any thought of meeting that person or persons involved brings on deep feelings of anxiety. I have seen church members who wanted to go to a fellowship, but skipped it because another Christian would be present. Almost invariable they would say, "I do not have a problem with them, I just don't want to be around them." If these smaller conflicts are not dealt with they do not diminish but grow until they produce anxiety. Hopefully each of you should have resolved these conflicts by the time you read this chapter. However, if they still exist it must be dealt with before you can have peace with God.

Unreachable standards

Some believers tend to be perfectionists. They set high goals for themselves, which cannot be attained. A failure to reach these goals may create frustration, a denunciation of self and develop anxiety. I met a young lady that had set such a high standard, that when she failed to attain the standard she had an emotional breakdown. She could not forgive herself. It took months for her to regain her confidence spiritually. The desire to be accepted is one of the underlying reasons for perfection and for setting high standards. When any believer sets too high a standard for themselves, it is often to seek approval and acceptance. There is nothing wrong in setting a high standard, but it should never exceed God's standard.

What causes anxiety is allowing the standard to rule and control one's emotional behavior, creating many kinds of emotional conflicts. Others may set the standard a person attempts to live by and the failure to live up to the standard may create a number of emotional reactions including anxiety. For a Christian this conflict is compounded, when people fail to live up their own standards. There is no inner peace. Self is holding self's feet to the fire. If a person fails to live up to God's standard the Holy Spirit convicts, confession is made and inner peace returns.

Unattainable desires

These desires may include power, prosperity and popularity. These desires are stirred up by the success of others, lust or greed, etc. Many believers have become hooked on the attainment of some household item, a car, a stereo, and even a mate. It seems that society thinks that the person who buys the last toy wins. The failure to attain dreams is taken by individuals, consciously or subconsciously as an attack on their person. These desires tend to possess their thinking to the degree, that the failure to achieve their desires is to be a failure. It seems to impart the idea that I am less important than my neighbors. If the neighbor is not a believer it compounds their thinking.

The book of Job addresses this problem. The question is, "Why do the wicked prosper and the righteous suffer." I've seen TV evangelists proclaim God doesn't want a believer to be poor. Prosperity or the lack of it does not depend on claiming something by faith. This passage definitely negates this type of thinking. Jesus said, *"Do not lay up for yourselves treasures upon earth."* Needless to say this passage in Matthew is aimed at the desires of an individual. The desire of a Christian should be to, *"seek first His kingdom and His righteousness; and all these things shall be added to you."* Matthew 6:33.

Uncontrollable problems

In the series of commands in this passage, Jesus was apparently describing one of life's problems, the fear of poverty. He said, *"What shall we eat? Or what shall we drink? Or with what shall we clothe ourselves?"* In a believer's life many problems may arise such as, sickness, death, divorce, financial failure, loss of a job, and a host of other problems. Problems may come as a flood, and a believer seems engulfed with no end in sight. Job is an example of someone facing unlimited problems. The life of Job and God's response to him is an example to teach all believers to trust in the Lord. In the end after losing everything, God blessed Job and He will bless all those who are faithful. The blessings may not result in the accumulation of wealth, but will include God's love, mercy, grace and His continual presence. Any believer that keeps his focus on his problems and not on God can move into a state of anxiety. A focus on problems can create anxiety, while a focus on God alleviates anxiety.

Be honest why should a Christian worry about problems over which he or she has no control. The solution to the problem is the Lords. If a believers attempts to control an uncontrollable problem he is acting as his own god. You might say, "You mean I do not have to do anything." No, keep reading and find the solution.

Unconfessed sin

A believer may ignore God's conviction about sin, and continue in sin. But while this is happening the Holy Spirit will prick the conscience bringing about a conviction of sin. As a result, emotional conflicts arise out of this anxiety about one's relationship with God and begin to control the mind. Disobedience to God creates an awareness of sin, which may create an emotional backlash which may lead to anxiety. The Psalmist said, "*When I kept silent about my sin, my body wasted away.*" Psalm 32:3. The Psalmist suffered physical consequences as a result of unconfessed sin. Physical problems may arise from emotional problems. Even when sin is confessed and a believer fails to accept God's forgiveness and cleansing; this failure to forgive one's self can create anxiety. A failure to accept forgiveness is a sin. It is playing god in your life. Recognize trusting God in forgiveness may run counter to the emotional self, this is why it takes faith.

CONSEQUENCES OF ANXIETY

The physical consequences

Anxiety robs one of energy. A day of anxiety is harder than a day of hard labor. Nehemiah said "*...do not be grieved for the joy of the Lord is your strength.*" Nehemiah 8:10. Anxiety depletes your strength while joy supplies strength. Anxiety destroys cells in the brain and affects the organs in the body. It may shorten your life span. It also creates stress, which harms the body. Some of the physical symptoms of anxiety are, headaches, heartburn, fatigue, sleeplessness and hyperventilation, to name just a few. Books have been written on this subject. If you are suffering physical problems, read and determine if it is anxiety related.

The emotional consequences

Anxiety not only attacks the body but also the emotions. It destroys a logical process of thinking. It allows anxious thoughts to dominate and control. These thoughts will push out other thoughts, which threaten their existence. Anxiety gains support from other emotions such as fear, anger and depression. These emotions are yoked together. The more anxious one becomes, the greater the impact upon the emotions. They become more unbalanced. Anxiety becomes a controlling force. Some other symptoms of anxiety are, emotional upheaval, panic attacks, fearfulness, and nervousness to name a few. Remember anxiety is an enemy of faith. Anxiety is self-seeking. It is a failure to be filled with the Spirit of God.

The spiritual consequences

The most destructive part of anxiety is its effect on a Christian's relationship with God. It destroys your faith in God. It amplifies unbelief. Thus, anxiety is a sin. It destroys a believer's fellowship with God. Since anxiety is focusing on self rather than God, it is placing self on the throne of your life rather than the Lord. It is reliance upon self rather than trusting God. Anxiety is an overt act of unbelief, and is an act of disobedience, which results in a breach of fellowship with God. Anxiety robs a believer of inner peace. It is as if a believer is saying to the Lord, "I cannot trust You to take care of my every need and every problem, I have to work these things out for myself." When a believer commits his troubles to the Lord, Paul states that God's peace stands guard over the heart and mind. Philippians 4:7. Anxiety is addressed again in Chapter 10.

Freedom from Anxiety

FREEDOM REQUIRES A SEARCH FOR GOD

Seeking requires a command

Jesus expresses freedom from anxiety. He said, *"But seek first His kingdom and His righteousness."* "Seek" is a present imperative. It is a command to continuously seek God's kingdom and righteousness. It is to "seek first," not second or third. Seeking is the desire for the primary or supreme and to place all other matters in a subordinate role. The Lord did not say seeking was preferable rather it is primary. It is in the present tense, which indicates believers are to continuously seek the kingdom of God. In order to obey this command, it demands a commitment. It is a commitment to seek God's control over your life. The prerequisite for God's control is regeneration, the new birth. An unbeliever does not have the Holy Spirit as a guide. He is under the control of the flesh, the world and the devil.

Seeking requires a commitment

The command requires a commitment to seek the character of God on a daily basis. Jesus said, *"But seek first His kingdom and His righteousness."* This means seeking God's purpose as well as God's person. The purpose in seeking *"His kingdom and His righteousness"* is to place everything in the proper perspective. Only the things of God are eternally important. Thus it is taking your eyes off the temporal and placing them on the permanent. The nature of man is to seek the temporal and ignore the spiritual. Jesus commanded the disciples *"Do not lay up for yourselves treasures upon earth..."* His reasoning was, *"... for where your treasure is, there will be your heart also."* If a believer treasures God's kingdom and His righteousness, that will be the focus of his heart, not the treasures of the earth. When a believer follows this command with a deliberate decision to follow God, God will then place within the heart the desire to seek Him.

Freedom requires a submission to God

Submission requires humility

Peter wrote, *"Humble yourselves therefore, under the mighty hand of God, that He may exalt you at the proper time, casting all your anxiety upon Him, because He cares for you."* *"Humble yourselves"* is an aorist imperative. The aorist indicates a decisive act not a gradual process. It is adopting an attitude of accepting God's sovereignty and of man's total submission. Anxiety is an open admission of self-exaltation. It is rebellion against God's sovereignty. Jesus said of Himself, *"Take My yoke upon you, and learn from Me, for I am gentle and humble in heart, and you shall find rest for your souls."* Matthew 11:29. When He said he was gentle and humble in heart, this did not mean He was a pansy. Paul describes Jesus' submissive attitude in Philippians 2:5-11. Believers are commanded, *"Have this attitude in yourselves which was also in Christ Jesus...but emptied Himself, taking the form of a bond-servant... and being found in appearance as a man, He humbled Himself by becoming obedient to the point of death, even death on a cross."*

Submission reveal His mighty power

Believers are instructed to humble themselves, *"under the mighty hand of God."* Submission is recognizing that God has a purpose in all things, and an acceptance of that purpose. It is an attitude of dependency upon Him in all things. It is allowing God the freedom to act on your behalf. It is standing still and seeing the might of God at work. Submission is an acknowledgment of God's power and sovereignty at work in the world and particularly in one's life. Paul describes this in Ephesians 6:10-17. Paul states in verse ten of this chapter, *"Finally be strong in the Lord, and in the strength of His might."* **A believer is only as strong in the Lord as the level of his submission.** Strength comes from God. Submission is the key to unlock the cell doors, which anxiety imposes upon the believer.

FREEDOM REQUIRES SUPPLICATION

Prayer is required

Paul wrote about this topic, *"Be anxious for nothing, but in everything by prayer and supplication with thanksgiving let your requests be made known to God."* Philippians 4:6-7. There are two imperatives in this verse. The first is *"be anxious for nothing."* It is a present imperative, a command with continuous action. The second is *"be made known."* It is a present passive imperative. The command forbids anxiety but demands prayer. Anxiety develops as one allows thoughts to erupt and begin to control one's attitude, activity, and actions. God's solution for the believer is to pray. Instead of the soul attempting to solve the unsolvable, prayer diverts the problem to God. The passage mentioned earlier in I Peter 5:7 confirms prayer. Peter wrote, *"...casting all your anxiety upon Him."* One of the old hymns carried this message, "take your burden to the Lord and leave it there." True prayer is a conscious releasing of the burden to God's care.

Most Christians are aware their problems are the Lord's. They attempt to lay them down, but immediately pick them up. Laying them down is done by faith. Picking them up is an act of the mind. Problems may need to be laid down fifty times a day, if so do it. This is an act of the will, in obedience to the Lord. The emotions will attempt to stake a claim on this pit of garbage, and the believer must develop the habit of resisting their undue influence. When the mind picks up what the spirit of a believer lays down it is an act of the flesh. In Galatians Paul wrote about the flesh, *"For the flesh sets its desire against the Spirit, and Spirit against the flesh; for these are in opposition to one another, so that you may not do the things you please."* Galatians 5:17.

Prayer is rewarded

The reward of submission and supplication according to Paul is, *"And the peace of God which surpasses all comprehension, shall guard your hearts and your minds in Christ Jesus."* As a result of unloading the burdens, which cause anxiety, God will grant inner peace. That peace will guard the soul, which is the mind, will, and emotions. This does not mean that a believer will understand the problem, but it does reveal that a believer accepts God's sovereignty over the problem and has inner peace. Society attempts to escape from anxiety by using pills, drugs, alcohol, pleasure, vacations, buying sprees, etc. Believers should use God's escape from anxiety; which is faith and trust in Him. Faith in God is best expressed through prayer and waiting on God. When a Christian prays he is saying, Father I am giving you my concerns and my cares. I trust You to accomplish what You desire through these troubles in my life to make me a better person."

Real Life Illustration

A female believer was prone to panic attacks brought on because of anxiety. These emotional cave-ins would bring a short hospital stay. She could not stop worrying. As a result of the continued discipline in controlling the thoughts and a total commitment to God, she gained victory over anxiety. The principle used to win over anxiety was illustrated in chapter two. In counseling she was asked many times; "If she was a living dead person and all of life's problems were the Lords, then when she fretted over them was she acting as her own god." She was prone to take a burden to the Lord, leave it for a few minutes, and then pick it up again. This is typical of those who are worrywarts. This is a simplified conclusion of her victory after many days of reckoning the self-dead to feelings of anxiety. No emotion which controls ones life can be controlled in a minute. It takes days and weeks to be victorious.

Verbal Commitment to the Lord

Father I confess it is so easy to get trapped in focusing on worldly matters rather than seeking first Your kingdom and Your righteousness. I now commit before others that I will not allow the cares of this world to create a climate of anxiety. I have sinned in the past by carrying my own troubles and worrying over future things. I have acted in unbelief I now state verbally that this was sin and I choose to walk in faith. I ask You to convict me in the future when I allow anxiety to create an attitude of unbelief.

Thought Provoking Questions

1. Are believers in general preoccupied with the cares of this life? Is the conversation and expression of joy of most believers over things rather than the Lord and His work?

2. Should Christians deliberately deed over to God, self, family, car, home, furniture, checking and savings accounts or in essence all they possess? What does this indicate?

3. Can a person express anxiety and be filled with the Spirit? If not; why not?

4. Do most believers have a disposition to worry and complain in the midst of real or assumed problems? Do they also have a habitual anxiety over how things will work out? What should their response be?

5. Why should a believer rejoice in all things?

---

† Warfare Prayer

Father, I confess the sin of anxiety. I accept the following scripture, *"...do not be anxious for your life, as to what you shall drink, nor for your body, as to what you shall put on. Is not life more than food, and the body than clothing... but seek first His kingdom and His righteousness, and all these things shall be added to you."* Being anxious is not seeking your kingdom, forgive me for the sin of anxiety. Teach me how to withstand the attack of the wicked one in this area. I know that some of the fiery darts sent my way are anxious thoughts. I will reject those thoughts, express praise to you for what you are doing in and through my life. I recognize that Satan would like for me to question Your purposes in life. By faith I accept that You will cause all things to work together for good. I refuse to worry about those things, which are under Your control.

STEPS OF ACTION

- Resolve each morning and periodically through the day to focus on God's person, and to relegate any anxious thoughts to God through prayer.

- Memorize Matthew 6:33 and make it your watchword. When anxious thoughts begin to assault your mind, quote this verse until they subside.

- When worry arrives, ask yourself the following questions, Am I occupied with the cares of this life? Is my conversation and expression of joy over things rather than the Lord and His word? Does anything mean more to me than living for and pleasing the Lord?

- Deliberately deed over to God on paper if needed, yourself, family, home, car, furniture, savings account and all you assume you own. State the following, by this act of my will, I acknowledge You as Lord over all You have given me to oversee. It all belongs to You, even if I didn't acknowledge it. I am acting in harmony with Your will. I commit myself to remember this concept of ownership, and I invite the Holy Spirit to convict me when I assume an attitude of ownership.

- Ask yourself after deeding over to God all you have, the following question. "Do I have an inner peace and confidence that God will work out every problem?" If the answer is no, renew your commitment to the Lord until peace comes.

Chapter 9

&

Unholy Fear Under Control
1 John 4:18

The following are a few questions which need to be answered before a believer begins this study. Be honest and answer each question without supposing what God would have you write.

1. What is the one thing that terrifies you?

2. When does fear become a sin?

3. Is fear the opposite of faith?

4. Is it a sin to be fearful when your life is threatened?

5. How can fear be turned into spiritual growth?

Introduction

All emotions have a positive as well as a negative side. Love, for example, is to be self-sacrificing, but if carried to the extreme in relation to self, it turns into selfishness. Fear is a positive emotion given to man for his protection and good. It was also designed to be used to reverence and fear God. It is wise to have a healthy respect for a rattlesnake or any dangerous animal. However, when the sight of a snake in a cage terrifies a person, it indicates fear is out of control. The Lord also desires awe or fear in respect for His person. This awe and reverence is called *"the fear of God."* This fear cannot be separated from faith and trust in God. Actually, the more one trusts in God, the greater the reverence and honor. As man's faith decreases, often-negative fears increase. Negative fears are usually based on false assumptions. An acronym for fear would be **F**alse **E**vidence **A**ppearing **R**eal. There is no one alive who has not experienced fear. It is a normal emotion. However, abnormal fear must be actively resisted rather than pursued. The greater one fears, the less practical is his or her life.

Fear robs believers of self-assurance, a positive self-image, and confidence in spiritual relations, emotional maturity, physical health, etc. This passage in I John 4:18 states, *"Perfect love casts out fear."* Perfect is used in the sense of mature. This simply means growing into a self-sacrificial love for God, which develops spiritual maturity thus fears of any magnitude will not distract from a faith life.

> **Text**: *"There is no fear in love; but perfect love casts out fear, because fear involves punishment, and the one who fears is not perfected in love." 1 John 4:18.*

The Prevailing Pattern of Fear

A PRINCIPLE ABOUT FEAR

A principle regarding fear could be described, "unrealistic fear is an illusion built up in the mind, thus appearing real." As the mind continues to chew upon these thoughts which promote fear, the thoughts become reality and fear sets in. A proverb which is so true states, "As a man thinks in his heart, so is he." Proverbs 23:7. The nature of fear is to promote more fear. The mind may say, "There is no reason for me to be afraid." Yet fear will continue to control one's emotions and thoughts. Fear is a normal reaction and a godly emotion.

Adam and Eve were afraid of God because of their new awareness of sin. The problem is not fear itself but abnormal fear. It is these abnormal fears which need to be brought under control. Someone might say to a person with abnormal fear, "Stop fearing there is nothing to be afraid of." This seems to be an easy solution, however it is easier said than done. Major fears and phobias must be dealt with over a period of time.

Phobias are strongholds and must be dealt with as a stronghold. See the chapter on Strongholds.

A PROJECTION OF FEAR

Most of the things which create abnormal fear are normal viewed by a biased mind. They are not seen from God's perspective. *"Perfect love"* is seeing things from God's viewpoint.

Fear of dying

Fear of dying is a type of abnormal fear, which may be the result of many terrifying experiences. It may be the result of not being saved; it may be a lack of confidence and trust in God and one's salvation. The following are scriptures that combat these issues. *"Even though I walk through the valley of the shadow of death, I fear no evil; for Thou art with me."* Psalm 23:4. *"And do not fear those who kill the body but are unable to kill the soul; but rather fear Him who is able to destroy both soul and body in hell."* Matthew 10:28. *"The fear of the Lord prolongs life, but the years of the wicked will be shortened."* Proverbs 10:29. Some people so fear dying that they will not discuss the subject. This should not be the attitude of a believer. Paul said, *"We are of good courage, I say, and prefer rather to be absent from the body and to be at home with the Lord."* 2 Corinthians 5:8.

Fear of failure

Fear of failure limits believers in attempting projects, and it roots into a poor self-esteem. Many people will not further their education or search for a new job, because of this fear. The theme song for this type of people is, "I could never do that." They are enveloped in the security blanket of failure, never attempting new things for fear of failing. The psalmists said, *"Though a host encamp against me, my heart will not fear. Though war rise against me, in this I will be confident."* Psalms 27:3. This fear is often an out growth of the rejection of self. All mankind has failed to live a life acceptable to God. God provides a new life where one cannot fail, as long as things attempted will bring glory to God. If a believer develops the attitude, that I am living this life to the glory of God, why should they fear failure? God is displeased when believers are fearful of failing and do nothing. Jesus gave believers assurance of doing great things. He said, *"Truly, truly, I say to you, he who believes in Me, the works that I do shall he do also and greater works than these shall he do; because I go to the Father."* John 14:12.

Fear of rejection

Fear of rejection is another fear which fruits can deter a fruitful spiritual life. A complete chapter has been devoted to the attitude of rejection. If this is one of your fears read the chapter. The root of feeling rejected is a poor opinion of self-worth. The attitude may be, "I don't want to go, people won't like me." Remember the first chapter indicated all Christians are clay and God is the potter. Anything irritating in life is allowed to be there by the Lord to make the believer more mature. The psalmist said, *"The Lord is for me; I will not fear. What can man do to me?"* Psalms 118:6. A believer should remember that the Lord does not reject His children. All rejection is self-imposed. Any so-called rejection by others is the means by which God can grow a believer into a life of faith.

Fear of sickness

Fear of sickness often creates anxiety over the future. An innate fear of suffering and dying from some terminal disease has burdened the minds and emotions of many believers. Over the years this writer has met a number of believers who believed they would suffer the debilitating effects of cancer. This so possessed their minds and emotions that it tainted their view of God's providence. Jesus said, *"Are not five sparrows sold for two cents, and yet not one of them is forgotten before God. Indeed, the very hairs of your head are all numbered. Do not fear; for you are of more value than many sparrows."* Luke 12:6-7. Fear of some terrible physical problem is failing to trust in God's love and protection.

Fear of poverty

Fear of poverty has driven many people to hoard up food and possessions. Depression years have built in older people this fear. Store up for tomorrow for there is coming another day. There is nothing wrong in saving for a rainy day. This is godly wisdom. However, when this so dominates a believer's thoughts that it destroys trust and dependence on the Lord, it is sinful. The psalmist wrote, *"O fear the Lord, you His saints. For to those who fear Him, there is no want."* Psalms 34:59. In another psalm he wrote, *"He has given food to those who fear him."* Psalm 111:5. A proverb states, *"Better is a little with the fear of the Lord than great treasure and turmoil without it."* Proverbs 15:16. This type of fear plays into the hands of Satan. Satan knows when believers have an abnormal fear of the future; they are in effect controlling their own life, rather than trusting in God. Jesus deals with this extensively in the Sermon on the Mount.

Fear of the future

Fear of the future is common. "What is going to happen to me?" is one of the questions asked by many people. Fortunetellers line their pockets because of this curious desire. However, this natural curiosity when carried to the extreme can devastate a person. Part of the passage used previously does apply to this fear, *"Indeed, the very hairs of your head are all numbered. Do not fear, you are of more value than many sparrows."* Luke 12:7. The tendency for most people is a desire to have a road map for the future. They desire to know what is going to happen, when and how it will happen. As fear of not knowing develops, it leap frogs into a fear of future unemployment, health risks, college costs, etc. These can be normal until they captivate your thinking and begin to control ones actions. James wrote regarding life, *"Come now, you who say, 'Today or tomorrow, we shall go to such and such a city, and spend a year there and engage in business and make a profit.' Yet you do not know what your life will be like tomorrow. You are just a vapor that appears for a little while and then vanishes away. Instead, you ought to say, 'If the Lord wills, we shall live and also do this or that.'"* James is indicating believers should live a life trusting in the Lord, rather than self.

Fear of false gods

There is a fear of false gods. I have seen believers who were frightened of demons to the degree, that they did not want them mentioned. False gods have demonic power as their basis for existence. There should be no abnormal fear of the devil much less false gods. Note how Jeremiah described false gods, *"Like a scarecrow in a cucumber field are they, and they cannot speak; they must be carried, because they cannot walk! Do not fear them."* Jeremiah 10:5. Most believers would deny fearing of false gods or demons. However, they would never stand up against the enemy of Christ, Satan. Many Christians attribute to Satan, godly powers. He does not have any of the attributes of God. He is not all knowing, all powerful or everywhere at the same time. John, the disciple of Jesus, wrote, "*...greater is He who is in you than he who is in the world.*" 1 John 4:4. In America, the problem is not false gods but demonic spirits. Christians are fearful of demons or evil spirits, which is seen by their actions. The projected attitude often is, "I don't want to make them mad at me." John wrote about the mission of the Lord, which should be the desire of every believer. His message is, *"The Son of God appeared for this purpose, that He might destroy the works of the devil."* 1 John 3:8. Instead of fearing the forces of evil, Christians should be storming the gates of hell. This is the message Jesus gave Peter *"...and upon this rock I will build My church; and the gates of Hades shall not overpower it."* Matthew 16:18.

A PROCESS OF FEAR

Physically

Fear begins with a thought, either real or imagined. As these fear thoughts multiply, they create physical reactions such as sweaty palms, the energizing of the body, and chill bumps. Intense fear can even cause death. Fear can cause a person to freeze and not be able to move, or explode in a frenzy of anger, and action. The physical reaction is usually brought on by the emotions.

Emotionally

Fear can erupt in anger, frustration, and anxiety. Fear can so captivate one emotionally, that when the apparent danger is past, fear continues to exist. Children and adults, who are awakened with nightmares, have difficulty removing the thoughts and fears from their minds and emotions. This emotional reaction is good, unless it is the result of excessive fears.

Spiritually

Unbridled fear ultimately affects a believer spiritually. Elijah's reaction to Jezebel's threats revealed how fear can affect a Christian spiritually. This was detailed in the chapter on depression. If fear is allowed to control your emotional behavior, it will result in the sin of unbelief. The children of Israel feared the inhabitants of Canaan and thus, did not believe God and failed to enter the land. The result of their unbelief was to wander in the wilderness for another thirty-nine years. The same is true for believers; fear may cause them not to inherit God's Promised Land. <u>This Promised Land is a life of faith</u>. It is not an exclusion from heaven. Abnormal fear in the face of God's leadership can result in missing Gods blessings. Joshua testified about fear by saying, "*Nevertheless, my brethren who went up with me made the heart of the people melt with fear...*" Joshua 14:8. The text for this exposition states, "*Perfect love casts out fear.*" This is relying upon God's leadership in every situation and making fear take a back seat.

A PERCEPTION OF FEAR

Fear carried to the extreme becomes a phobia. Phobia comes from a Greek word *phobia*, which is translated fear. *Agoraphobia* is the fear of the marketplace. Agora is the Greek word for market. Sin is at the root of all phobias; the sin of unbelief, resentment, bitterness, etc. Often counselors desire to alleviate this suffering, by teaching and training the patient to cope. They assist in unlearning a habitual reaction of fear. However, Satan can attack by oppressing an individual in the area of weakness, thus compounding the strength of the phobia. Since fear is unbelief, it allows Satan to attack.

Paul wrote, "*Be angry and yet do not sin, do not let the sun go down upon your anger and do not give the devil an opportunity.*" Ephesians 4:26-27. The word opportunity in the Greek means place or location. The failure to forgive allows the forces of evil to attack a Christian emotionally.

Real Life Illustration

As mentioned previously a 21 year old Christian lady, who had been in counseling for four years for agoraphobia, desired to be set free from this emotional handicap. Through an interview it was determined the root of the problem was the failure to forgive her father for divorcing her mother. After she dealt with the sin of resentment, she could not be oppressed by the wicked one and was set free from agoraphobia. It is not always easy to destroy a phobia, but it can be done through an application of the truths found in this book. Phobias can be based on sin which is used by the forces of evil to launch an attack on a believer.

A Proper Perspective of Fear

THE PRINCIPLE OF FEARING GOD

The fear of God, seen in its proper perspective, is awe, or a reverence towards. Wuest states that it is, "a controlling motive of the life, in matters spiritual and moral, not a mere fear of His power and righteous retribution, but a wholesome dread of displeasing Him." It is the ultimate in belief. The awe and reverence of God should direct believers in their daily activities. It is one thing to believe with the mind and another to act on your belief. Suppose a famous person who had previously jumped a number of semi trucks asked the audience, "Do you believe, I can jump 15 trucks with someone on the motorcycle with me?" The crowd roars its approval thus believing it can be done. Then he asks, "Who will be willing to make the jump with me?" It is one thing to believe with the mind, it is another to believe with the inner part of man. The believer should reject fears and have faith in God. Jesus told His disciples, *"And do not fear those who kill the body, but are unable to kill the soul, but rather fear Him who is able to destroy both soul and body in hell."* Matthew 10:28.

THE PROMISES FOR FEARING GOD

There are numerous scriptures, which relate God's promises to those who fear, (reverence) Him. Some of these are, *"The angel of the Lord encamps around those who fear Him."* Psalms 34:7. *"You who fear the Lord, trust in the Lord; He is their help and their shield."* Psalm 115:11. *"For as high as the heavens are above the earth, so great is His loving kindness toward those who fear Him."* Psalm 103:11. The Bible is filled with promises to those who give God their life, and cast all their cares, including fear, upon Him.

THE PICTURE OF FEARING GOD

Jesus is the pattern, set by the Father, for believers. He is described in Isaiah 11. This passage is messianic and pictures the life of the Messiah, Jesus. Note what the prophet wrote, "... *the spirit of knowledge and the fear of the Lord. He will delight in the fear of the Lord...*" Jesus reverenced and respected the Father. He did nothing without the Father's permission. Jesus was not frightened of the Father, but displayed reverence and respect. This should be the attitude of every believer. Near the end of Jesus' ministry the Father approved of Jesus life when He said, "*This is My beloved Son, with whom I am well-pleased; listen to Him!*" Matthew 17:5. When a Christian allows the Spirit of God to control life's problems they are living a life of faith and following Christ's example.

THE PEACE WHICH COMES IN FEARING GOD

When Christians place their trust in the Lord, peace is the result. When Paul wrote to the Philippians, he was aware of their destitute condition. They were in deep poverty and were being persecuted. He wrote this promise to assuage their fears, "*And the peace of God which surpasses all comprehension, shall guard your hearts and your minds in Christ Jesus.*" Philippians 4:7. In this passage God's peace is pictured as a soldier standing at the gate of a walled city. God's peace is standing guard over the believer and will not allow fear to enter into the walled city of his heart and mind. The peace of God is the opposite of fear, since it is an expression of faith. It is a fruit of the Spirit. When fear monopolizes the lives of believers, they are not under the control of the Holy Spirit. The fruit which appears is the works of the flesh as described in Galatians 5. Overcoming abnormal fears will bring inner peace and a deeper faith in God.

THE PRACTICE OF FEARING GOD

Fear of the wicked one and the common fears of life can be controlled through a **realization of God's power**. As has already been mentioned but so true is Jesus warning to His disciples. He said, "*But I warn you whom to fear; fear the one who, after He has killed, has* *authority to cast into hell; yes, I tell you, fear him."* Luke 12:5. Satan does not have this authority only God. Believers are under the watchful eye of God. There is a hymn entitled "His Eye is on the Sparrow." This hymn gives assurance of the ever loving care of God. The psalmist said, *"The eyes of the Lord are toward the righteous, and His ears are open to their cry."* Psalm 34:15.

A second necessity in overcoming fears is **recognition of His person.** When a believer fears things, situations, problems, prospects for the future and numerous other things, more than God; he has in effect, made them god. If fear is master over a Christian, fear has become god. Jesus said, *"No one can serve two masters..."* Matthew 6:24. If fear is master over a believer, God is not. The command to the nation of Israel was, *"And now Israel, what does the Lord your God require from you, but to fear the Lord your God, to walk in all His ways..."* Deutermony 10:12. The Lord desires believers to walk according to His standard, and to trust in His providential care.

In addition to overcoming fear it is essential to **recognize God's purpose** for life. One of God's purposes for man is living a holy life. Excessive fear focuses on the flesh (soul) and sin. Excessive fear takes the Lord off of the throne of your life and replaces God with self. This makes excessive fear ungodly or sinful. Paul admonishes believers about the flesh. Note what He wrote to the Corinthians. *"Therefore, having these promises, beloved, let us cleanse ourselves from all defilement of flesh and spirit, perfecting holiness in the fear of God."* 2 Corinthians 7:1. Paul gave a warning to the church at Ephesus, which applies, to all Christians. *"Therefore be careful how you walk, not as unwise men, but as wise, making the most of your time, because the days are evil."* Ephesians 5:15-16.

One of the ways to overcome excessive fear is to **accept the word of God.** This requires faith. The unwillingness to accept God's word is rebellion. Awe and reverence are directly in opposition to rebellion. The Lord gave the following instructions concerning God's word to the children of Israel. *"And it shall be with him, and he shall read it all the days of his life, that he may learn to fear the Lord his God by carefully observing all the words of this law and these statutes."* Deutermony 17:19. This command was to hear, accept and practice God's word. God desires not only an agreement with His word but the practice of it. Some readers will argue about some of the statements I've made. This is the way it is with God's word. Even those who accept it as infallible have difficulty accepting that it will apply in their particular situation.

A second suggestion in overcoming excessive fear is the **application of God's word**. Application of the word is a faith walk. A life of faith will encounter trials, problems and fears. If it did not, it would not require faith. Paul encourages the believer to take their problems and fears to the Lord in prayer. Once they are given to the Lord, they should be forgotten. *"Be anxious for nothing, but in everything, by prayer and supplication, with thanksgiving, let your requests be made known to God."* Philippians 4:6. These suggestions seem so simple yet so difficult to implement. Later in this chapter as in all of the chapters, steps of action will be given which will assist in growing into maturity

Real Life Illustration

A lady with an abnormal fear of small spaces and the fear of heights was set free from this fear. As a child she was locked in a closet. Her parent forgot her and she became terrified. This and other events made her an extremely fearful person. She had a fear of failure, of people and even of God. She had to allow her mind to relive some past experiences, write them down on paper and thank God that He kept her safe during these traumatic experiences. As a result of rethinking fearful experiences and praising God for them she was set free. Needless to say she also confessed the sin of unbelief, for failing to trust God in everything. The stronghold of fear was destroyed. Fear at times would raise its ugly head and attempt to reclaim its emotional hold. It was necessary to continue standing in faith, declaring her to be free from the power of this emotion. As months flew by she became totally free. Reviewing the past and confessing away the base for a stronghold is to remove the power attached to a traumatic experience which will set free the mind and is part of the renewing process as described in Romans 12:2.

Verbal Commitment to the Lord

I confess that my desire is to respect the Lord to have a holy awe about His person and work. I refuse to allow any kind of earthly fear to dominate and control my emotions. I acknowledge fear carried to the extreme may become a phobia. If I allow fear to control my emotions, it means, I have sinned against the Lord. I realize my past reactions to fear are buried in the subconscious, and when certain stimulus arrives my current reactions are based on past reactions. I wish to destroy the power of fear over my emotions based on previous actions. I choose to act in faith and love. The Lord is my shield and I will hide behind His divine protection.

Thought Provoking Questions

1. Ask yourself, what kind of creatures do I fear? Is it a fear of snakes, spiders, bugs etc? Is this type of fear normal? If so, then what makes this fear sinful?

2. When a believer is so fearful of heights, an elevator ride brings panic, is this normal? If being in public creates abnormal fear is this a sin?

3. What makes fear a sin?

4. What is the opposite of fear?

5. How can the emotion of fear be godly?

6. In your personal opinion can a person defeat the power of fear without God's help?

---

† Warfare Prayer

Father, I confess the fear of (identify the fear or fears). I ask your forgiveness for the sin of unbelief revealed by this fear. I realize that I am allowing fear to control me. Therefore, in essence this makes fear my god. I ask to be free from the spirit of fear. I will allow the Holy Spirit to remind me of the occasions of past fears, and I will confess them. I also ask the Holy Spirit to renew this area of fear in my mind and emotions. I am trusting in your word, *"There is no fear in love; but perfect love casts out fear, because fear involves punishment, and the one who fears is not perfected in love."* Father, I refuse to allow the emotion of fear to become my god through its control. Fear in control is the flesh warring against the spirit. I choose to *"stand in the strength of your might."* As I review past emotional experiences, I ask you to destroy the power behind them so my mind and emotions can be set free.

STEPS OF ACTION

- Look at present and past fears, determine their source and strength. Write them down. Ask God for forgiveness for those, which prompted you to sin. Ask God to cleanse the subconscious from the power of these fears.

- Memorize I John 4:18, and apply it to any excessive fear that attempts to dominate your emotions.

- Any phobia must be dealt with as a stronghold. Review the lesson on strongholds and implement the steps of action.

- Confess any carnal fear. This may include a fearfulness that someone will offend and drive off a prominent member of the church or a compromising attitude because of the fear of rejection.

- If the awe, reverence or fear of the Lord is absent from your life, begin pursuing God with your whole being until this becomes a reality. It is almost impossible to destroy a stronghold of Satan built on fear until a stronghold of reverence for the Lord is built.

Chapter 10

&

A Spiritual Response to Emotional Problems
Philippians 4:4-9

The following are a few questions which need to be answered before a believer begins this study. Be honest and answer each question without supposing what God would have you write.

1. What should a believer do when it seems life is out of control, when everything is going wrong?

2. Can a Christian overcome the trauma of emotional conflict?

3. How do the demonic forces of evil discourage Christians through the emotions?

4. How can a believer be victorious over the powers of darkness and the work of the flesh?

Introduction

Before we study some other emotions it is time to reflect and review what has been learned in a practical way. In Philippians 4:4-8, Paul sums up a believer's response to emotional conflict, physical ailments and any and all circumstances. This passage, in effect, sums up all of the previous expositions on the control of emotions. It contains all of the positive elements, which enable a believer to overcome. This passage in Philippians is an exhortation to the believer on "how to overcome." Paul wrote about this church at Philippi in his letter to the Corinthians, "... *that in a great ordeal of affliction their abundance of joy and their deep poverty overflowed in the wealth of their liberality.*" 2 Corinthians 8:2. Paul wrote this letter to the Philippian church which was poverty stricken and afflicted. His solution to their problem was to command them to follow certain procedures. The guidelines encouraging the Philippians, as found in this passage, can be applied to almost everything disrupting a believer's life. Paul recognized the need to overcome fleshly emotions which war with the spirit of a believer and the Spirit of God. This passage, if applied, will assist the believer in living above emotional conflicts. The title of this chapter indicates that I believe there is a spiritual response to most emotional conflicts. This response requires a Christian to act in faith.

> *Text: Rejoice in the Lord always; again I will say rejoice! Let your forbearing spirit be known to all men. The Lord is near. Be anxious for nothing, but in everything by prayer and supplication with thanksgiving let your requests be made known to God. And the peace of God, which surpasses all comprehension, shall guard your hearts and your minds in Christ Jesus. Finally brethren, whatever is right, whatever is honorable, whatever is lovely, whatever is of good repute, if there is any excellence and if anything worthy of praise, let your mind dwell on these things. The things you have learned and received and heard and seen in me, practice these things and the God of Peace shall be with you. Philippians V-9 4:4-9.*

The Premise of Faith

THE COMMAND TO REJOICE

The definition of rejoice

The word *"rejoice"* is a present imperative. The present tense calls for a continuous and habitual activity of rejoicing. This continuous command to rejoice expresses a mandate for the believer. Joy is the opposite of depression. Joy is that inner relationship with God, which is a result of fellowship with Him. Often joy must be declared by faith, before it becomes a reality. Since joy is a fruit of the Spirit, it will be present in fullness when a believer is filled with the Holy Spirit. As one walks by the Spirit, he receives the joy of God. Not only are Christians commanded to rejoice, they are instructed to *"Rejoice in the Lord."* When circumstances and problems seem to inundate a believer, the focus of joy is to be placed in the Lord. He is the Lord of all problems. Paul wrote, *"Be anxious for nothing."* Rejoicing should take place in little trials as well as major trials.

The design of rejoicing

"In" is in the locative tense and indicates rejoicing is in the realm or sphere of the Lord. When the children of Israel were marching around Jericho, they were told to put the ark out in front. They were to focus on the presence of the Lord rather than the impenetrable walls of Jericho. Focusing on the Lord makes the impossible, possible. Paul reinforces this command by repeating, *"...again I will say rejoice!"* An old chorus describes this truth, "Turn your eyes upon Jesus, Look full in His wonderful face and the things of earth will grow strangely dim in the light of His glory and grace." The design of joy is to look at life's problems from a higher plane. The emotions tend to view problems from the level of the flesh, rather than the throne of God.

The duration of rejoicing

How long should a believer act by faith and rejoice? Paul wrote, *"Rejoice in the Lord always."* The Greek word for *always* is in every case translated always. This means the believer is to rejoice in the Lord twenty-four hours a day. This would mean seven days a week, and fifty-two weeks a year for life. When a believer acts in faith, there should be no circumstance or problem, which would keep him or her from rejoicing in the Lord. Rejoicing allows the believer to be on top of difficulties and problems, instead of under them. It is much easier to see the wisdom and will of God while looking down on the trial, than from under the problem. Problems may create a variety of emotions, which if left unabated will cause confusion, doubt and anxiety. It is easy to rejoice when things are exciting with no problems on the horizon. However, problems are the opportunities, which lead to rejoicing. As rejoicing takes place, excessive negative emotions will abate.

IT INVOLVES A COMMAND TO FORBEAR

The definition of forbearing

As has been shown rejoicing reveals an attitude of faith. Paul added another element of faith. He wrote about forbearance, *"Let your forbearing spirit be known."* *Forbearing* is a combination of *epi*, upon, and *eikos*, reasonable. The preposition stresses the intensity of reasonableness. It is translated as forbearance, gentleness and sweet reasonableness. This passage could be translated "to have a sweet reasonableness in judging, trials, events, problems and people." This is the opposite of a haughty, argumentative, touchy kind of disposition. Christians are challenged to let forbearance be known. *Be known* is an aorist passive imperative. The aorist would indicate that one's life, in its totality, would be one of forbearing. Since forebearance is an imperative, it commands us to live victoriously under the trials of life.

The declaration of forbearing

Paul declares a Christian's forbearance should be recognized by others. The word *known* is *ginosko*, and signifies to be taken in knowledge, to come to know, recognize, understand, or to understand completely. This word is used for experiential knowledge. The believer's life should reveal a meek and gentle spirit, not only toward self but also toward others. Any person who insists on expressing his rights does not have a forbearing spirit. Even unbelievers, who are encountered in life, should identify a believer by a forbearing spirit. Forbearce requires a walk of faith.

The Plan of Faith

ADOPT THE RIGHT ATTITUDE ABOUT PROBLEMS

Faith and anxiety cannot co-exist. Doubt and anxiety are bosom buddies. Paul admonishes the Philippians, *"Be anxious for nothing."* As seen in the chapter on anxiety, *"anxious"* is *merimnao*, which signifies to be anxious about, to have a distracting care. It is a present imperative. With continuous action, it would indicate that one should habitually adopt a life style of refuting anxious thoughts. Paul issues this as a command. This command is all-inclusive since Paul adds *for nothing*. Paul used a broad stroke and included anything and everything facing a believer in his life, when he used "for nothing." This means that no situation, no matter how trying or desperate, should drive one into anxiety. Anxiety is the opposite of peace and joy. When one rejoices in the Lord, feelings of anxiety disappear. A Christian cannot be filled with joy and be depressed and anxious about life's problems. Actually, I believe a Christian cannot be filled with the Holy Spirit and allow anxiety and depression to oppress through the emotions.

ADOPT THE ATTITUDE OF PRAYING

The magnitude of prayer

Paul does leave Christians with an alternative. The alternative is faith praying. He wrote, *"...but in everything by prayer and supplication with thanksgiving let your requests be made known to God."* When Paul wrote *but in every thing*, it indicates a believer should take every problem, no matter how small, to God. The tendency for most Christians is to take problems to the Lord when they seem to be insurmountable. In reality, when a believer is born again, he exchanges his life for Christ's life. Paul wrote, *"I have been crucified with Christ, and it is no longer I who live, but Christ lives in me; and the life which I now live in the flesh, I live by faith in the Son of God."* Galatians 2:20. Since the believer's life is Christ's life, each believer should learn to trust and lean upon Him. There is no problem communicated to the Father, which would cause Him to frown upon the believer. Instead, it stirs up His love. Parents would be distraught if their children were having problems, which could not be solved by the child but could by a parent, and the child would not allow the parent to help with the problem. So it is with God as Father. He desires that His children call upon Him. Remember there is no problem too big or too little for God.

The motive in prayer

Paul wrote, *"By prayer and supplication with thanksgiving."* Paul makes one stipulation in letting the Father know about your concerns. The stipulation is with thanksgiving. Thanksgiving is a combination of *eu*, well, and *charizomai*, to give freely. The attitude in prayer should be an expression of gratefulness and thankfulness for God's past and present mercy. It is an appreciation for His love and grace. The attitude of thanksgiving places God in the proper position of honor and reverence. Many believers pray, almost cursing God for current trials, thus elevating the self. When a Christian is grateful, it elevates God and dethrones self. One might say, I am not grateful, because I don't feel grateful for what is happening. Gratefulness and joy, often requires an act of faith. It is confessing gratefulness when the emotions express other feelings. This is done over and over until the emotions come into harmony with the faith act of gratefulness.

The must of prayer

Prayers are to "Be made known to God." Made known is a present passive imperative; it is a **command** with continuous action. Paul commands believers to pray about their problems. The tendency is to tell everyone, including unbelievers, about your problems before they are related to the Father. Needless to say, the Father knows about the problems before a believer prays. A principle seems to exist, regarding prayer and a believer's needs. It seems the Father waits until a believer is desperate enough to pray before He moves on some problems. This principle develops maturity, trust and faith in believers. Some believers through their actions are saying, when all else fails, I will call on God. Christians should say, before I try anything else, I would try God.

ADOPT THE ATTITUDE OF PEACE

The potential of peace

"And the peace of God which surpasses all comprehension" indicates the mind cannot comprehend peace. The word surpass is *huperecho*, which is a combination of *huper*, above and *echo*, to hold. Thus, it is to be superior to or be better than. Paul states that God's peace will surpass, be superior to, or far greater than, man's ability to comprehend. The *peace* of God is that harmonious relationship between God and man. It is the absence of separation and the establishment of fellowship. Peace is the absence of conviction of sin. Peace is an inward awareness a believer is pleasing the Lord with his life. Since peace is a fruit of the Spirit, it comes when a believer is in the center of God's will. Unbelievers can never have inner peace. It is an established principle of a relationship God grants to believers. It can be fully accepted or partially rejected. Comprehension is *nous*, which signifies to perceive with the mind. It could be translated understanding. A man with a finite mind cannot understand nor comprehend the purposes of God, as they apply to life and its problems. The application of this truth is everything is under His control, when it appears there are no solutions to life's problems. This requires walking in faith. Remember faith believes something is so, when it does not appear to be so, in order for it to be so.

The purpose of peace

Paul also wrote the peace of God, *"shall guard your hearts and your minds in Christ Jesus."* "Guard" is *phroureo*, a military term, to keep by guarding, to keep under guard, as with a garrison. This is a picture of a soldier standing guard, perhaps at the gate of a walled city. This guard would control everyone who went in and came out. The phrase shall guard, is dependent upon the preceding exhortation of the Lord. Peace is His guard and when He gives it, it is a reminder that everything is under His control. This is a picture of the Holy Spirit guarding the believers heart (heart is the center of one's being) and the mind. The Holy Spirit does not grant inner peace when His instructions for receiving are ignored.

The prerequisite for peace

"Let your requests be made known." The Lord doesn't guarantee to protect your emotional being if the command to pray is ignored. The tense used with the word guard carries a promise of a continuous guarding. Peace stands guard over the heart. The heart is recognized as the center of your emotions and as well as the mind. The mind is the control center for thinking and controlling your emotions. God's peace does not promise to eliminate all excessive emotions or irrational thoughts. God's peace will protect your heart and mind from potential emotional conflict and from satanic attack. God's peace is available to every believer but can be accepted or rejected.

The Practice of Faith

THE CHALLENGE FOR RIGHT ATTITUDES

The command for right thinking

Paul gives a command for right thinking when he wrote, *"Let your mind dwell on these things."* The word "dwell" is *logizomai,* and means to reckon. In this passage dwell means, make those things the subjects of your thoughtful consideration or carefully reflect on them. Paul believed a believer could control the thought process. The Holy Spirit inspired him to write commanding believers to order their thinking on things, *"worthy of praise."* The present tense indicates believers should make this a continuous or habitual action. Paul orders believers to set their minds on heavenly things not the troubles and problems of life.

The characteristics of right thinking

Paul lists six characteristics of the kingdom that believers should allow to control their thought process. The first is *"whatever is true."* Often believer's thoughts are focused on a lie, not what is true. Any time a believer is so focused on a problem and is weighed down by that problem, he is focused on a lie not truth. Jesus said, "I am the way, the truth, and the life." The next characteristic is *honorable*. Honorable in the Greek is *semnos*, that which is worthy of respect or honor, noble, dignified, reverent. This word carries the idea of that which is majestic and awe-inspiring. Negative emotions often carry a desire to demean the culprits rather than honor them. This shows dishonor to God. The third characteristic is *right*. "Right" is *dikaios*, and signifies righteous, a state of being right, or right conduct. The K.J.V translates it just. It is a wholesome appreciation of the right way of living and of life. It is not focusing on the evil of the world.

The mind should be focused on God's righteousness not the wickedness of man. The next characteristic mentioned is *pure*. "Pure" is *agnos*, and signifies to be morally pure, pure or undefiled. In the Old Testament this word would indicate ceremonial purification. In this passage it stresses the purity of life in one's attitude and actions. This is a reminder to live a holy life, reread Roman 12:1-2. The fifth characteristic is *lovely*. "Lovely" is a combination of a preposition, *pros*, toward and *phileo*, to love. It is translated pleasing, agreeable, or lovely. This is a concept from God's viewpoint not man's subjective reasoning. A tree may be lovely but who would focus on a tree. This is a focus on the benefits of a grace life, such as heaven, the coming of the Lord, salvation, and God's grace and mercy. The final characteristic is to be of *good repute*. Good repute is a combination of *eu*, meaning well and *pheme*, a saying or report. It is translated a good report, good reputation or good repute. If believers listen to good reports instead of bad, it will enable them to control their emotional reactions. Reports, good or bad, trigger thoughts which trigger an emotional reaction. These reports are to be well sounding, praise worthy. Have you listened to a false report about yourself or a friend? Did this false report stir up an emotion of anger, resentment, envy, or perhaps jealousy? If yes, your mind was focused on an unworthy event.

Paul used two first class condition phrases when he wrote, "*if there is any excellence and if anything worthy of praise.*" If in this case doesn't mean maybe so or maybe not. The literal translation of this first class condition is since. It is to be taken as an actual fact. It means of course there is excellence and of course there are things worthy of praise. Excellence denotes moral goodness, virtue. In this passage it means moral excellence. Paul exhorts the believer to focus on eternal qualities rather than temporal oddities. He challenges the believer to *let your mind dwell on these things.*

THE CHALLENGE FOR RIGHT ACTIONS

The context for right actions

The challenge Paul laid down was, *"The things you have learned and received and heard and seen."* These four terms describe the perimeter of their practice. Paul indicated that a believer was responsible for the light received. *Learned* is truth put into practice. This word is akin to the word for disciple, a learner. *Received* is truth passed down through teachers, family or tradition and accepted by an individual. The last two *heard* and *seen* probably refer to those truths taught and shown through the life of the apostle. This forms the basis for Paul's next thought of practicing these truths. He limits their responsibility to known truth. A believer is not responsible for unknown truth.

The command for right actions

The admonition is to *practice these things*. Practice is *prasso*, and means to do, to practice. In Paul's writings, this word denotes a habit. Paul is exhorting the Philippians and believers of all time to develop a habit of doing these things. Practice is a present imperative. The present tense calls for a continual habit of doing. As an imperative it is a command, with the continuing results of acting in obedience. Practice indicates a daily walk. Most believers can practice these truths when things are going smooth however let rough times come and they have difficulty with them. The control of a Christian's life begins with controlling the emotions. The truths set forth in this passage, if practiced faithfully, will mature believers in their walk with God. No one can live a life where the flesh does not prevail on some occasion, but this should not keep them from trying. Paul said practice these things. I believe, as a ball player must practice in order to become an accomplished player, so Christians must also practice Christian living. Paul gave a promise, which comes as a result of practicing faith. He stated, *"And the God of peace shall be with you."* This is reaffirming God will bring peace to a troubled heart. It is a promise of His recognized presence.

Paul was writing this letter to the Philippians while in prison. Paul knew he was facing some difficulties and was having a difficult time but was reluctant to share this with the church at Philippi. He wrote, *"Now I want you to know, brethren, that my circumstances have turned out for the greater progress of the gospel."* Philippians 1:12. He was indeed rejoicing in

154

all things. Therefore he could encourage the church at Philippi to rejoice and believers today to *"rejoice in the Lord again I say rejoice."*

Verbal Commitment to the Lord

Father, I confess the sin of allowing the problems of the world to rob me of joy. I commit myself to a moment-by-moment habit of praising You in all things. I will also through prayer make my requests known to You. I know to praise You in all things is to walk by faith. I commit myself to a faith walk. My desire is to be filled with joy, not self-pity. I ask for You to stand guard over my mind and heart. I will begin to practice those things, which I have learned, received, heard and seen.

Thought Provoking Questions

1. Is there anything, which has occurred in your life for which you have difficulty in praising the Lord?

2. Do your prayers reflect more on self than on the problems of others?

3. Do you feel the peace of God guarding your life?

4. How does the inner peace take the place of emotional troubles?

5. How does rejoicing in all things express faith?

6. Does praising God about a problem condone the sin connected with the problem?

---
† Warfare Prayer

Father, I thank You for (describe the problem). This problem did not catch You by surprise. So by faith, I know You will work this together for good. In this matter and in all things I rejoice and give praise and thanks. I refuse to allow the forces of evil to gain any ground in my life by refusing to be joyful. I ask for Your peace to stand guard over my heart (emotions) and mind and thus protect me from the work of the devil.

STEPS OF ACTION

- Begin each morning by setting aside the day as one to rejoice in. Begin by playing praise music, singing praise songs, reading a psalm, and spending time in a daily devotion.

- Recognize rejoicing in the Lord usually requires an act of faith. Two examples of expressed faith is rejoicing when the emotions want to cry, or forgiving when the emotions wish to retaliate. Remember that faith is rejoicing when you do not feel like rejoicing, so that you may feel like rejoicing.

- Develop the habit of taking every problem to the Lord in prayer, and leave it there. A common problem is to take a problem to the Lord and not leave it to the Lord's direction. The problem is we don't, we pick it up. Tell the emotions and self a hundred times a day, if necessary, I will not worry or fret over God's problem. It is His and I will not play God by dealing as god with His problem.

- If you do not have inner peace with the Lord, then sin needs to be confessed. Ask the Lord to reveal the sins, which keep you from having fellowship with Him. One of the primary sins that keep believers form having inner peace is unbelief. Unbelief keeps believers from praising God in all things.

- Practice thinking on things, which edify, rather than on temporal things.

Chapter 11

‽

Rejecting Feelings of Rejection & Overcoming Guilt.

Ephesians 1:3-6 Romans 8:31-39

The following are a few questions which need to be answered before a believer begins this study. Be honest and answer each question without supposing what God would have you write.

1. Do you ever feel rejected when someone doesn't speak to you or you are ignored?

2. Is there ever an occasion in which you feel rejected without any reason?

3. Do you have guilt feelings over some past sin, which has been confessed?

4. Can someone make you feel guilty because you did not live up to their expectations?

Introduction

This study will be about two different topics. They differ from each other but are entwined as a rope. They are *feelings of rejection* and a *guilt complex*. Rejection of self is a rejection of God's handiwork, which may bring about feelings of guilt. Also feelings of guilt can feed feelings of rejection. If rejection of self is still a problem read Chapter 1.

Rejection is an emotional feeling arising out of a poor self-appreciation. This is not an emphasis on establishing a good self-esteem.

Rather it is a reminder of the truths taught in Chapter 1. Remember we are God's creation and should accept ourselves as His perfect gift to ourselves. Feelings of rejection are allowing the soul man to control the emotions. Guilt is the soul man allowing the emotion of guilt to control and when it does, guilt becomes a person's god. This will be explained in more detail. If a Christian has guilt feelings and there is no accompanying conviction from the Holy Spirit, reject those feelings.

The text should be read over and over until you know who you are in Christ. The text will show how this study on rejection and guilt is contrary to God's word. Note Paul asks, "who is the one who condemns?" It is impossible for self or someone else to separate a believer from the Lord.

> ***Text:*** *"Blessed be the God and Father of our Lord Jesus Christ, who has blessed us with every spiritual blessing in the heavenly places in Christ, just as He chose us in Him before the foundation of the world, that we should be holy and blameless before Him. In love He predestined us to adoption as sons through Jesus Christ to Himself, according to the kind intention of His will, to the praise of the glory of His grace, which He freely bestowed on us in the beloved." Ephesians 1:3-6. "For whom He foreknew, He also predestined to become conformed to the image of His Son, that He might be the first-born among many brethren; and whom He predestined, these He also glorified. What then shall we say to these things? If God is for us who is against us? He who did not spare His own Son, but delivered Him up for us all, how will He not also with Him freely give us all things? Who will bring a charge against God's elect? God is the one who justifies; who is the one who condemns? Christ Jesus is He who died, yes, rather who was raised who is at the right hand of God, who also intercedes for us. Who shall separate us from the love of Christ? Shall tribulation, or distress, or persecution, or nakedness, or peril or sword?" Romans 8:29-35.*

The Actions Feeding Rejection

AN ATTACK ON ONE'S PERSON

The attack can involve physical abuse

Physical attacks may include beatings, hunger, imprisonment, sexual molestation and many other acts of violence. This type of abuse prolonged over a long period leaves emotional scars. It brings about thoughts of unworthiness and self-rejection. I experienced this type of physical and mental abuse. When a parent tells a child they will never amount to a hill of beans, it creates a feeling of rejection. A parent who slaps the face of a child communicates I can't stand the sight of you. The world is full of people who were physically abused and turned against society and are now imprisoned. This topic does not need to be explained in detail since it is so evident in our cities and streets.

The attack can involve emotional abuse

Parents are destructive when they use graphic statements, which create feelings of rejection. Some of these are, "I hate you. I can't stand the sight of you. I wish you had never been born. Aren't you ever going to grow up?" These kinds of statements make the abused feel that acceptance and love is conditional on right responses. Emotional abuse is almost as destructive, if not more so, to one's emotional well being as physical abuse.

> Real Life Illustration

A lady having attempted suicide was placed under my counseling. Under hypnosis with previous counselors, she could not recall anything before 12 years of age. In the next chapter we will explain the principal of the Holy Spirit bringing out of the subconscious past thoughts and how to be set free from them. After preparing this lady to accept herself and accept that God loved her we asked the Holy Spirit to open her mind and allow the past to be seen so that the things occurring in past times affecting present reality could be dealt with. She agreed and the Lord brought to her mind terrible memories. At three years of age she was used in sexual intercourse with a dog. Many of these type things occurred until she was 12 years old. At 12 she was in the hospital with a miscarriage and her father was warned if this ever happened again he would go to jail. After facing the past absolving herself from the guilt and rejection she was freed. Today she lives a normal life. However the scars of the past remain. Often as with this lady, the abuse was emotional, sexual and physical.

An assumed attack on one's person

The equating of a person with performance

Parents often approach discipline with their children with statements such as, "You are a bad boy. The way you approach life, you will never amount to anything." It would be better to say, "You are a good boy, but you did a bad thing." Parents should separate a person from their performance. Usually parents treat their children as they were treated. Recently I was told of a young man who was a troublemaker in school. He said no one wanted me in the class. I made terrible grades. When I entered high school, a teacher took me aside and instead of scolding and threatening me, began to complement me. The end result I became an honor student and went to college. What made the difference? There is an old saying "You can catch more flies with honey than with vinegar."

It is imperative believers treat their children with grace. In a previous chapter we used the passage in Ephesians 4:29. Paul wrote, *"Let no unwholesome word proceed from your mouth, but only such a word as is good for edification."* Edification means to build up not tear down. Parents and friends are notorious in tearing down a person's self worth and failing to edify their children. Children make many mistakes, but so do adults. Aren't you glad that God does not treat his children they way adults treat their children.

The expressing of one's person as valueless

When a parent throws a temper tantrum over a broken dish, it communicates to the child, "the dish was more valuable than you are."

It would be better to say, "I am sorry that a dish was broken. However, it can be replaced, I am happy that you didn't get hurt." Otherwise parents place a higher value on things than their children.

A former member did not want any more children, and she became pregnant. All through the pregnancy she resented the child. When it was born she treated the little girl with disdain. She was destroying the child's self worth. After listening to a message on the sovereignty of God, she confessed the sin of mistreating the daughter and a young lady was saved from the entire events which occur when there is a lack of self worth. **Self worth is not self esteem.** Self worth is seeing self from God's perspective.

The emergence of one's person as being unloved

When abuse occurs, thoughts begin to possess a person's mind. They begin to think like the following, "I can never please my parents, and they don't love me. My parents hate me, since they never show me any affection. If I left they wouldn't care." This type thinking is usually untrue. Most parents love their children, but do not know how to show it or express it. I felt unloved for years. There was no tenderness shown to me as a child or an adult. I could never remember being kissed or hugged by my mother or father. This developed into an inferiority complex, which revealed itself with an attitude of superiority. As a grown man finding my worth as shown by God's word, I could look into a mirror and look eye to eye with my negative feelings.

The Attitudes Feeding Rejection

THE DESIRE FOR APPROVAL

The desire for approval is found in small children. When they do something, clap for them and watch their reaction. Note *the desire for approval is giving by God to everyone.* My grandchildren have reacted positive when they see adults approving their performance. In fact, they continue their behavior to get this approval. This is a God-given desire, unless it is carried to an extreme, then for adults it can become sin.

Often this desire for approval makes a young adult adopt unrealistic attitudes. Subconsciously they are motivated to gain acceptance through performance. When this fails, it compounds their feelings of unworthiness.

I have seen children hide their report cards from their parents because they do not want disapproval. Children will keep some important items from their superiors because they fear disapproval. Recently a young man quit the football team without asking his parents and became a team manager. His parents were upset with him because he quit without asking their permission and for not telling them he quit. However, the young man was afraid to talk with them about the problem for fear of disapproval.

THE DESIRE FOR ACCEPTANCE

Rejection causes pretty girls to think of themselves as ugly. The internalized presence to conform to a peer group is a result of the need for acceptance. *This need for acceptance is also godly unless it is carried to an extreme.* When anyone feels they must conform to a lifestyle or mode of dress to receive the approval and acceptance of a peer group, this reveals a weakness in self worth. If someone needs to feel good about self, they substitute the opinion of man and the world for God's. God gives the desire to be accepted and loved. There is nothing wrong with this concept unless it changes your opinion of God or makes a person do something ungodly. The best way to raise a child is to teach them the truth explained in Chapter 1. Teach them to say I am a person or worth and value. God loves me and I accept myself as God's perfect gift to myself. I thank God I am who I am.

THE DESIRE FOR APPRECIATION

It seems the more one feels rejected the greater the need to feel appreciated. Remember a feeling of appreciation comes from the Lord. The desire for appreciation seeks affirmation after completing a task. Statements such as, "Did you like the dress I bought you?" "Have you worn the dress yet?" "Did anyone comment on how pretty it was?" One of the most common expressions around Christmas is, "Did you like my gift?" *The desire for appreciation is a God given trait.* God desires His children to appreciate and give thanks for His gifts to them. However, when appreciation is needed to anoint your ego it is wrong. I suffered from a lack of self worth and in my early pastorate desired earnestly to hear words of commendation. Needless to say, this was not trusting in the Lord. When every thing is said and done what really matters is God's approval. The Father said about Jesus, *"This is My beloved Son in whom I am well pleased."* I long to be pleasing to the Lord.

THE DESIRE FOR LOVE

Innate within all people is the desire for love. It is a God given quality. People will go to great extremes to fill this vacuum of love. A story is told that Hitler desired to find the language of a super race of Germans. He had children so isolated that no one spoke to them or showed them love. They were never held or caressed. The story relates that the children died. Love needs more than an object; it needs a person to return love. God is love. He so loved the world or mankind; He sacrificed Himself for man's sin. The greatest commandment is to love God. This desire when not met will cause many problems for teens as they seek love someplace besides home and the Lord.

The word love has been abused. A teen will say, "I love my car." How can you love something, which has no feelings? Love needs a response. Parents should reassure their children they are loved and especially before and after they are disciplined.

The Answer to Feeling Rejected

AN ACCEPTANCE OF GOD'S PURPOSE

In order to break the mind set of rejection and its emotional ramifications, it is essential to look beyond one's self. God's love for mankind was made in eternity past. God the creator of angels, earth, and the heavens chose believers to be His children. This makes them valuable and loved. They become the children of the Lord of lords and the King of kings. Why not ask, "Why does God love me and why am I alive? 'What is His purpose for my life?'" Rather than spend time wondering about your emotional self and who you are as a person, attempt to project yourself into God's thoughts for your life. What does He expect of you today? Read Chapter two on the sovereignty of God and find that you are to die to yourself and live to God. You no longer live, but God lives in you. Repeat, "I accept God as Lord of my life and whatever happens to me today, it is in the permissive will of God, and I thank Him for it before it happens."

AN ACCEPTANCE OF ONE'S POSITION

One of the most difficult concepts for a child of God is to accept that they are heirs, joint heirs with Christ. One of the many ways to determine if a believer accepts their position with Christ is prayer. Anyone, who doesn't think God hears his prayers, doesn't really believe they are fully accepted by God. Ask yourself these questions. "Do I feel loved by God? Will God answer my prayer as quick as a church staff member?"

When a believer is born again the Spirit of God changes his inner being. In the following passage, Paul writes abouts a deep truth. *"Therefore if any man is in Christ, he is a new creature; the old things passed away; behold new things have come."* 2 Corthians 5:17. The Bible calls believers' saints or holy ones. At salvation we entered into a spiritual kingdom. This makes this earth a temporary dwelling place. Our residence is in heaven. We have rights as one of God's children. In the book of Hebrews believers are encouraged to *"draw near with confidence to the throne of grace."* Rejection is seen in believer's prayers. They may say, "I know I don't deserve anything but could you etc." This is contrary to God's desire. Can you imagine a son or daughter coming home from school each day and asking permission to enter the house, to eat dinner or go to bed? As Christians we act as if we are not loved by God and don't belong to His family.

AN ACCEPTANCE OF ONE'S PERSON

This emphasis is expressed in the first chapter. It would be good to review its content. One of the ways to check your acceptance of yourself is to evaluate the following, Suppose you are at work or come in from school, and for no reason you are castigated, berated, cursed out and told you were a fool. How would you feel? Would you feel rejected? If the answer is yes, then you are normal. However, if the rejection remains and creates negative feelings, you have enthroned self and dethroned the Holy Spirit. Can you look at yourself in a mirror and appreciate who you are and thank God for all things?

The Application in Feeling Rejected - Romans 8:29-35

THE CATEGORIES OF GUILT

The scriptural view of guilt

Guilt as used in the New Testament means to bring a charge against, or to come forward as an accuser against someone. As seen in the text, guilt should come as a result of an accusation by God. Paul wrote, "*Who shall bring a charge against Gods elect?*" Feeling guilty is not always because a believer has sinned. The natural feeling of guilt should be defined as God bringing a charge. The correct term for guilt on behalf of a Christian is being convicted. The Holy Spirit working through the inner man brings an awareness of sin. After the sin is confessed the inner feeling of conviction will be lifted.

Adam and Eve had a sense of guilt or conviction when they disobeyed God. The resulting action depicts conviction. Adam and Eve could not stand in the presence of the Lord as they had at other times. In Genesis 3:8, "*They heard the sound of the Lord God walking in the garden in the cool of the day, and the man and his wife hid themselves from the presence of the Lord among the trees of the garden.*" Can you imagine someone attempting to hide from God? Guilt or conviction faces two decisions, one is to hide the sin and the other is to confess the sin.

The secular view of guilt

Webster Dictionary defines guilt as, "The fact of having committed a breach of conduct, especially such as violates law and invokes a penalty." The world looks at guilt from a different perspective than from a heavenly point of view. Guilt is a feeling or a failure to live up to the expectations of someone. As laws or rules are set, any violation of those laws or rules creates the possibility of guilt. This may include a breach of ethics, moral failure, or a failure to measure up to the expectations of another person. Guilt is described as a feeling of unworthiness, sinfulness, or failure arising from a variety of sources. Guilt may bring emotional reactions such as, a feeling of impending punishment, a feeling of unworthiness, a feeling of rejection or a feeling of failure. Needless to say this does not exhaust the emotional reactions to guilt.

Guilt can become such a stronghold in a person's life until life is not worth living. Later in this chapter an explanation will be given on how to deny guilt unless it arises from the level of a person's spirit. Non-Christians can have compounded guilt until they take their own lives. Christians should not suffer in this manner since the Lord paid the price for all sin and whatever is not sin should not produce guilt.

THE CAUSES OF GUILT

Guilt arises from sin

Everyone is born with a sin complex. Sin carries with it a guilt factor. Salvation brings peace from the guilt of sin. Joseph's brothers had feelings of guilt years after they sold him into slavery. Notice what the Bible relates about their sin. After they discovered Joseph was second to Pharaoh in Egypt they said, *"Truly we are guilty concerning our brother, because we saw the distress of his soul when he pleaded with us, yet we would not listen; therefore this distress has come upon us."* Genesis 42:21. They had never confessed the sin against Joseph to their father Jacob. As part of the punishment for their sin they were accused of being spies and thrown into prison.

Their comments were, *"truly we are guilt concerning our brother, because we saw the distress of his soul when he pleaded with us, yet we would not listen; therefore, this distress has come."* Can you imagine their chagrin when they had to tell their father Jacob that they deceived him years before? Unconfessed sin will always find the sinner out. Numbers 32:23 makes this statement regarding a commitment of two tribes, *"but if you will not do so, behold, you have sinned against the Lord, **and be sure your sin will find you out."*** It is impossible to hide sin from God. Guilt arises when a believer attempts to hide his or her sin.

Guilt arises from self

A guilt complex tends to create guilt as a form of self-punishment. This can be the result of a wrong concept of God or a twisted approach to one's self regarding a wrong concept about God. A person may feel God could never forgive, love or care about them after they committed a paticular sin. In addition, after confession of sin, they may have difficulty accepting God's forgiveness. To have a guilt complex is a failure to forgive yourself after confessing to the Lord and holding your feet to the fire for past deeds. This results in an act of self-punishment. A failure to accept God's forgiveness automatically triggers guilt feelings. Why is it so difficult to accept God's forgiveness for some sins? Society has taught most people that punishment for deeds come about as a result of a failure to live up to the laws of society. It is difficult not to transfer this concept to God. A Christian must realize that punishment for sin did take place. The Lord's death on the cross, paid for the sins of man. When a believer punishes himself or herself it is double jeopardy.

Guilt arises from someone else or Satan

It is relatively easy to put sensitive believers on a guilt trip. All that is needed is a forceful accusation for their failure to live up to or abide by the accusers standard. Most believers have a desire to please others, especially those they respect or in a position of authority. When an authority figure appears displeased with a person's performance it can produce guilt feelings. Note: if guilt arises and there is no inner confirmation from the inner spirit of a believer brought about by the Holy Spirit, it should be immediately rejected. By allowing guilt feelings to exist is to validate the accusation. It is allowing someone else to be your god.

Demonic spirits can also bring accusations against believers. The term, devil means to accuse, to malign. Years later, after a sin has been confessed, the forces of evil will bring to mind a particular sin, and with it a flood of emotions, which make a believer feel unforgiven. The accuser is attempting to defeat a believer and render him or her useless. Remember if the Lord has forgiven the sin and you allow the forces of evil to use it against you, it is nothing less than allowing them to be your god. A fact, which could be repeated many times, is **God sets the standards by which a Christian should live. If a believer fails to live up to that standard he or she has sinned. However, if guilt arises in a believer and there is no accompanying conviction from the Lord, then a believer is allowing self, someone else or Satan to put him or her on a guilt trip. This guilt trip is in itself a sin against God. It is allowing someone or something besides the Lord to be your god.**

Even when sins have been confessed, there is often an unwillingness to forgive oneself, or to see oneself without yesterday's wrongs. The following statements reflect this attitude, *"I can't believe I did that!" "I could shoot myself if it would do any good." Paul wrote, "Forgetting what lies behind and reaching forward to what lies ahead."* Philippians 3:13. A Christian cannot change the past, but he or she should not allow the past to negatively effect the present.

The Cure for Guilt

A DECISION OF ACCEPTANCE

An excessive feeling of guilt is a denial of God's divine purpose for believers. Paul wrote, *"For whom He first knew, He also predestined to become conformed to the image of His Son."* Romans 8:29. The divine purpose for believers is to be like Jesus. It is not God's purpose for believers to be controlled by guilt, rather by the Holy Spirit. In this same passage in Romans it indicates believers are justified which means to be declared righteous. If God has declared a believer righteous, then guilt should have no foothold in waging war against one's person. Believers are declared not guilty by God and are joint heirs in the kingdom. The measure of a person must be measured from God's viewpoint, not mans. Paul asks in this passage in Romans, *"Who will bring a charge against God's elect? God is the one who justifies; who is the one who condemns?"* Indeed the Lord has already forgiven in terms of eternal salvation. For a Christian confessing sin is reestablishing fellowship with the Lord, not as a means to receive salvation.

A DENIAL OF ACCOUNTABILITY

Repentance of sin

When inner feelings of guilt or rather conviction arise as a result of a sin or sins committed, the Holy Spirit will bring a realization of the sin. Repent and confess the sin or sins and accept God's forgiveness. Often times the acceptance of forgiveness is accomplished only by faith. The soul man's tendency is to feel guilty. Remember faith, believe the sin is forgiven when it doesn't seem like it is forgiven, in order for you to come to the realization it is forgiven. From this point on, reject any guilt feelings brought on by self, Satan or someone else. Any time guilt raises its ugly head and there is no specific sin pointed out by the Holy Spirit, guilt has no reason to exist. Reject this guilt and praise God for His forgiveness and grace. Remember confession of sin is agreeing with God the particular sin is a sin. Repentance is godly sorrow about sin and a determination to depart from sin and to a desire to be restored to fellowship with God.

Rejection of Guilt

If guilt feelings arise, which are general in nature reject them. The Holy Spirit convicts a believer of specific sins. General guilt comes from self; other guilt feelings are the work of the demonic directly or indirectly. Guilt can be idolatry. As we wrote before, allowing guilt to remain and reacting to it without accompanying conviction of the Holy Spirit is allowing the guilt to be placed above God. It is setting a standard above God's standard. If it were below what God wished, He would convict. The lack of conviction by the Holy Spirit means a standard has been set higher than God's. The source of the standard may come from self. If this be the case self is acting as god. If the standard comes from others then self is allowing someone other than God to bring guilt. This is making someone else god. The accusation bringing on guilt could come from a demon. If guilt arises and remains because of a demonic attack, then the demon in effect has become your god. When you have unsubstantiated guilt, confess the guilt to the Lord and claim His peace.

Verbal Commitment to the Lord

I choose to express my acceptance of my person as God's perfect gift to myself. I know that the rejection I have felt from others should not influence my concept of my well being. I reject past and current feelings of rejection. I will not allow them to affect my relationship with God, self, family or friends. When these thoughts rise up in my mind and emotions, I will confess them away and praise God. I will continue to praise God until these negative thoughts are defeated. When guilt arises because of a committed act of sin, I will confess it and accept my forgiveness. I know the forces of evil love to remind me of past mishaps in order to destroy my relationship with God. They also desire to destroy my relationship with others and put me on a perpetual guilt trip. I refuse to give these forces of evil an avenue to attack because of feelings of rejection or guilt.

Thought Provoking Questions

1. What is the root problem, which brings forth feelings of rejection? If it is a focus on self, why is that so bad?

2. Does God ever feel rejected? If so, why isn't it a sin?

3. When does the feeling of rejection become sin?

4. Why can't the feelings of rejection be eliminated overnight?

5. If your emotions indicate a person is being rejected, does that make it true? If not, why? When is a continued feeling of guilt a sin?

6. How does feeling guilty when all sins are confessed constitute idolatry?

✝ Warfare Prayer

Father, I confess my feelings of rejection go contrary to your word. It in effect makes me reject what you created. By this I am saying, "You did a poor job in making me and You have allowed my life to be messed up. In addition, if I had the power, I would change things." I repent of the rebellious attitude and ask for Your forgiveness. I choose to forgive those who have hurt me, by rejecting me. I ask that You strengthen me, in order that I can have a change of mind about my person. Create in me a new mind and attitude. I do believe that You love me and hear my prayers. I reject the thoughts that fly into my mind from the forces of evil or from the subconscious, which places me on a guilt or pity party. I am an heir of the King and I accept this position. I recognize that if I fail to accept myself as created by God, I reject His authority. I ask that the Holy Spirit would immediately convict me of any sin committed. I will reject all other guilt not arising from sin. I choose to oppose the attacks of Satan by claiming Romans 8:33-34. *"Who shall bring a charge against God's elect? God is the one who justifies, who is the one who condemns?"*

STEPS OF ACTION

- Deliberately confront and examine the nature of self-negating thoughts. Ask questions such as; is this concept of my person a result of a mind set developed over a period of years?

- Determine that you will cease accepting thoughts, even when your emotions make them appear true. Remind yourself that the real truth lies in God's word and His love for man.

- Make a deliberate decision to cease self-condemnation for the failure to measure up to the expectations of others.

- Remind yourself every day, that God accepts and loves each believer. This does not mean that He approves of their sin. However, it does mean we should not reject what God loves.

- Ask yourself the following questions: Do I try to leave a better impression of myself than is strictly true? Do I exaggerate in order to impress others? Do I stretch the truth in order to gain approval? Are you more concerned about what people will think than what will be pleasing to God?

- Evaluate feelings of guilt and determine if they are sin driven. If so, confess the sin and accept God's forgiveness. Reject all guilt not associated with sin.

Chapter 12

—— ❧ ——

How to Destroy Strongholds

2 Corinthians 10:3-4 Joshua 5:13-6:10.

The following are a few questions, which need to be answered before a believer begins this study. Be honest and answer each question without attempting to determine what God would have you write.

1. Is there an area of your life in which you virtually have no control?

2. Do you have a besetting sin or a sin which keep occurring no matter how hard you try not to sin?

3. Is your life like a roller coaster or an elevator? Spiritually are you hot and then cold?

4. If you asked a close relative what is my worst sin problem? What would they say?

Introduction

A stronghold is any sin or sins in the life of a church or an individual, which keeps them from achieving a spiritual victory. It is a sin, which constantly overpowers. It is a sin over which there is little or no control. Many believers desire to walk in victory, only to be defeated with the same sin over and over again. Paul states in 2 Corinthians 10:3-4, *"For though we walk in the flesh, we do not war according to the flesh, for the weapons of our warfare are not of the flesh, but divinely powerful for the destruction of fortresses. We are destroying speculations and every lofty thing raised up against the knowledge of God, and we are taking every thought captive to the obedience of Christ."*

The battle for a godly life is not against men and women but within oneself. It is also against the powers of the evil one or demons. The demons can influence the life of a believer. **This influence is not being demon possessed but demon oppressed**. If the fight was only with the flesh the battle would be won much easier.

Strongholds in the Christian's life are located on the level of the soul. They exist as a habitual mindset, emotion or thought process. They have taken a person captive to obey the stronghold's desires. Some strongholds in a church and in a believer's life are pride, lust, greed, resentment, anger, hate, unbelief, an unforgiving spirit, a critical spirit, fear, rebellion, depression, and anxiety, to name a few. The text reveals believers can have victory over sin's strongholds. I will illustrate this passage in Corinthians with the fall of Jericho. Before God's people could have victory in the Promised Land, which is a type of the Spirit controlled life, a fortress or stronghold had to be conquered. To justify the Promise Land as a type of the spirit filled life is illuminated by how God treated his people. While wondering in the wilderness for forty years their attire did not wear out. He provided a cloud by day and fire by night. He provided food, water, and guided them day by day. As soon as they entered the Promise Land all of these daily extras provided by God, ceased. It now became a life of faith, so it is with the spirit filled life. Jericho's destruction is God's revelation on how to overcome the power of sin and of the forces of evil. The passage in 2 Corinthians indicates it is a spiritual battle. It is not a battle of the flesh. Paul wrote, *"Put on the full armor of God, that you may be able to stand firm against the schemes of the devil. For out struggle is not against flesh and blood, but against the rulers, against the powers, against the world forces of this darkness, against the spiritual forces of wickedness in the heavenly places."* Ephesians 6:11-12.

The spirit filled life is a life of faith. The destruction of a stronghold is a faith act. Before the children of Israel could occupy the land by faith, Jericho had to be destroyed. In every believer's life a Jericho or Jerichos must be destroyed in order to live a consistent life of faith. Although the passage found in Joshua 5:13-6:10 does not allude to the destruction of sin's fortresses, it is a type or a picture of the fortress of sin. The principles used in Jericho's destruction are a valid way of destroying a stronghold on the level of the soul.

Text: *"For though we walk in the flesh, we do not war according to the flesh, for the weapons of our warfare are not of the flesh, but divinely powerful for the destruction of fortresses."2 Corinthians 10:3-4.*

Text: *"Now it came about when Joshua was by Jericho, that he lifted up his eyes and looked, and behold, a man was standing opposite him with his sword drawn in his hand, and Joshua went to him and said to him, 'Are you for us or for our adversaries?' And he said, 'No, rather I indeed come now as captain of the host of the Lord.' And Joshua fell on his face to the earth, and bowed down, and said to him, 'What has my lord to say to his servant?' And the captain of the Lord's host said to Joshua, 'remove your sandals from your feet, for the place where you are standing is holy.' And Joshua did so. Now Jericho was tightly shut because of the sons of Israel, no one went out and no one came in. And the Lord said to Joshua, 'See, I have given Jericho into your hand, with its king and the valiant warriors. And you shall march around the city, all the men of war circling the city once. You shall do so for six days. Also seven priests shall carry seven trumpets of ram's horns before the ark; then on the seventh day you shall march around the city seven times, and the priests shall blow the trumpets. And it shall be that when they make a long blast with the ram's horn, and when you hear the sound of the trumpet, all the people shall shout with a great shout; and the wall of the city will fall down flat, and the people will go every man straight ahead." Joshua 5:13-6:10.*

The Reasons for a Stronghold's Destruction

ITS SINFUL POSITION

God told Moses and the leaders of Israel to utterly destroy the inhabitants of the land. A stronghold must be seen through the eyes of God's holy nature. A sin or a Jericho, which is a stronghold, keeps believers from walking with God and thus, achieving victory. A stronghold must be seen as utterly wicked and then completely destroyed. A Jericho, on the level of the soul, may be pride, envy, jealousy, fear, anger, resentment, an addiction or any combination of these and many other things. When one wishes to hold on to any part of a stronghold, it cannot be destroyed. Often people wish to destroy a part of their Jericho and retain other parts, which appear acceptable. Let the lesson of Achan's disobedience reveal how dangerous this is for a believer. Achan disobeyed God's command by coveting and keeping gold, silver and a mantle. The end result of this sin was death. In order to understand the wickedness of a stronghold it must be seen from God's perspective. God knew the people of this new land and particularly Jericho, could create future sin problems for Israel. Their destruction was to protect them from future sin. A stronghold may not seem to be wicked to the casual observer. However, from God's wisdom, it may be extremely wicked. Since strongholds are wicked, they must be utterly destroyed.

ITS STRATEGIC POSITION

From Jericho you could view the Jordan. Jericho was the center of traffic going from north to south and overlooked a fruit-bearing valley. In order to occupy the land, Jericho would have to be destroyed. Sin and Satan will use a believer's stronghold to keep that believer from walking in victory. Satan, will attack in the weakest area of a believer's life. A sin stronghold is sin compounded and built up over a period of time, usually years. It seems indestructible. It occupies a place in the believer's life which defeats all attempts to have a victorious walk. It is a guarantee for an elevator Christian life. Jericho was not hidden in some valley, but was visible and was in a strategic location on a hill. Believers do not have to search for a stronghold, they are always evident. It is that area of one's life, which is virtually uncontrollable. Remember Jericho was strategically positioned to control commerce. So it is with a stronghold of the soul it will control what happens in every day life.

The Revelation About a Stronghold's Destruction

IT DESTRUCTION IS BASED ON A DIVINE PERSON

When Joshua met the Captain of the host of the Lord, he was not mapping out a plan to defeat Jericho but searching for God's revelation. The Bible states, when Joshua was by Jericho, "*He saw a man standing with his sword drawn and asked, 'Are you for us or for our adversaries?*" Joshua 5:13. The response was "*No, rather I indeed come now as captain of the host of the Lord.*" Joshua 5:14. This was not a man or Joshua would not have been commanded to remove his sandals because he was on holy ground. This was the Son appearing in bodily form. It was not an angel since angels are not to be worshiped. He had a drawn sword, which pictured the war as belonging to God. In effect He said to Joshua, "It is not a matter of my being on your side, rather are you on my side?"

This was the first time God gave direct instructions to Joshua by using the form of a man. You might say, "so what?" **If Jericho's destruction did not have other implications, why did the Lord appear in this manner?** I believe it was to show all strongholds can be destroyed if they are in opposition to God. Jericho was an enemy of God. Its destruction was in accord with God's will and purpose. John said that Jesus came, "*... that He might destroy the works of the devil.*" I John 3:8. Destroying the works of the devil has been completed as a result of the resurrection. The Holy Spirit empowers the believer to destroy sin's stronghold. However, there must be a deliberate decision to ask the Lord's advice on its destruction.

Iᴛ DESTRUCTION IS BASED ON A DELIBERATE POSTURE

A posture of submission

The following passage illustrates submission, *"And Joshua fell on his face to the earth and bowed down and said to him, what has my Lord to say to his servan?"* Joshua 5:14. Since Jericho was God's problem, its defeat required submission. Submission to God is a necessary requirement in destroying strongholds. When a person says, "I don't need God's help in breaking this habit or overcoming this problem." This is a sure fire way to be defeated. The Lord desires submission. Submission is a requirement for resisting Satan. Submission is standing under the authority of God, and being totally obedient to His commands in daily living. James wrote, *"Submit therefore to God. Resist the devil and he will flee from you."* James 4:7. Most strongholds are not regulated by the power of the devil rather they arise from the flesh.

Satan uses a stronghold to attack the believer. If a Christian is unwilling to confess and turn from any sin, he is rebelling against God. This means the believer is not submitted to God. Submission is a willingness to confess your sin and weakness, employ God's power and exert the will power to do as God directs. Joshua was willing to implement God's plan. He did not question the plan's validity or the means by which it would be accomplished.

A posture of serving

The following verse reveals this attitude, *"Remove the sandals from your feet for the place where you are standing is holy."* The removal of sandals placed Joshua in a position of a slave. It revealed willingness to worship and to serve. Free men wore sandals slaves did not. The removal of his sandals revealed Joshua's inner motivation. This action, with his bowing, indicates an attitude of reverence and worship. Joshua could have responded, "I am the leader of the Israelite army." Instead this leader was required to become a servant. A servant attitude is recognition of God's sovereignty.

When a Christian wants to be victorious over a stronghold it requires a servant attitude. Had Joshua not humbled himself and sought divine direction, he would have been defeated. If a believer is not willing to make God the Lord of his life, and adopt an attitude of being God's servant it is unlikely that he will have victory. A servant does not argue with God over how the stronghold will be destroyed, rather he obeys God's plan. This does not mean that it is fully understood or that the believer is in agreement with it. It is adopting an attitude of; the boss said it and I will do it, no matter what.

ITS DESTRUCTION IS BASED ON A DIVINE PLAN

God's plan involves commitment

The Lord told Joshua *"See I have given Jericho into your hand, with its king and the valiant warriors."* Joshua could have said, "It looks to me like Jericho is still standing." The plan required Joshua and the children of Israel to act in faith on God's word. Joshua had to believe Jericho would be defeated, before it was defeated, in order to bring about its destruction. Joshua must have gathered the army together and revealed God's plan since it was implemented. Can you imagine the officers of the army indicating the plan would not work? In order to accomplish God's plan, Joshua had to be committed. He could not deviate from God's plan one iota. The Lord gave specific details and it would have been easy to say Why not change it in this area?"

When strongholds are to be destroyed, it requires a similar commitment to God. He desires the believer to be free from the stronghold of sin, but He requires a commitment, in order for the believer to be set free. It is a commitment to do as God directs without any shortcuts. Suppose Joshua had said, "I believe seven days are too many, I will march around for only five days." The walls would not have fallen and Israel would have attempted to destroy Jericho without God's help. So it is with sin's strongholds. The plan of God must be followed deliberately and completely.

God's plan involves courage and consistency

For six days Israel went out from their camp, marched around the city and went back to camp without speaking a word. The Captain of the host of the Lord said Jericho had valiant warriors. It is likely they verbally abused this army of Israel, which had no experience in destroying walled cities. Jericho felt secure behind its walls. It took an act of God for the walls to be breached. It is likely the soldiers in Jericho made slurring remarks, which could have angered the Israelites, and yet they kept quiet and marched around the city. In camp they could have said, this is stupid, we need to build ladders to scale the walls. Each day they marched around the walls tight-lipped, obeying the Lord. The seventh day God required them to march around Jericho seven times. This required even more courage and consistency. Believers have a tendency to want instant victory. This type of spiritual warfare indicates victory can come suddenly if the price of obedience and submission is paid ahead of time. If a Christian wants to be free from a stronghold of sin and will not follow the procedures God has set forth for it's destruction, he is acting foolishly.

Over the years I have seen people who desired instant victory without paying the price for victory. Take smoking for an example, often Christians want the Lord to immediately take away all craving for tobacco. The Lord is able to give this kind of victory. However, it is His desire to see believers walk by faith and grow in grace. He will allow baby Christians to struggle. Did you ever carry babies until they could walk on their own or did you allow them to learn how to walk? So it is with the Christian walk, the Lord allows believers to stumble in learning to live a godly life.

God's plan involves a cost

The passage reads, *"The wall fell down flat, so that the people went up into the city, every man straight ahead, and they took the city."* The destruction of Jericho required the effort of all the men of Israel. Once the walls fell, it was necessary to take the city by force. Believers often desire to defeat their stronghold without paying a price. God could have destroyed every inhabitant of Jericho without Israel's help, but He chose to make Israel pay the price for its destruction. Needless to say, some of the men of Israel died. This was the price for victory. So it is with a believer's Jericho. There is a price to be paid for its destruction. This cost may involve asking forgiveness of a spouse, a friend or the church. It may involve restitution, or giving something away. God will require the believer to become a living sacrifice. A living sacrifice was discussed in chapter two. Remember, Paul wrote, *"this is your spiritual service of worship."* Romans 10:1. Is there any worship without paying a price? Often the price is to be a living sacrifice.

It's Destruction is Based on Divine Principles

The principle of a siege

It takes time to destroy strongholds. Jericho is an example, *"Now Jericho was tightly shut because of the sons of Israel; no one went out and no one came in."* The children of Israel had laid siege to Jericho. It could not be resupplied with food, water, or other warriors. In order to destroy a stronghold, a believer must not allow it to be reinforced. If the stronghold is anger, then one must curtail anger. It is a resolve to destroy and not allow the stronghold to get stronger.

A siege weakens a stronghold, so that it can be defeated. Laying siege to an emotional stronghold is determining it will not gain strength through being used by the believer. Any time sin controls a believer it compound the influence of that sin. Sin compounds in the mind and emotions by developing habits of sin, destroying will power, searing the conscience and grieving the Holy Spirit. A siege stops this process. Strongholds begin at an early age, and develop to maturity as an adult. Since they have been erected over the years it may take more than a week to tear them down.

The principle of faith

As was mentioned, the plan for destroying Jericho required faith. The army marched around Jericho for seven days expecting God to provide a miracle at the conclusion of the seven days. Believers often want instant victory without paying the price of acting in faith. Why did the Lord make them wait seven days? Seven is a perfect number and can represent any number of days. Believers must lay siege by faith expecting God to provide the way for a Jericho's destruction. The faith of Israel was expressed by their actions for seven consecutive days. For all of Israel to walk around a city and not begin preparing the necessary weaponry to attack Jericho, reveals extraordinary faith. A believer also must be willing to march around his or her Jericho in faith until God brings the victory. Since seven is a perfect number, then the march of faith is that perfect number of days He selects. For some it may be one day and for others He may require a month or a year. Remember it took Israel forty years to reach Jericho from Egypt. Destruction of strongholds is by faith. This does not mean every person of Israel knew how God would bring victory. It does not mean there was no doubt.

Faith is acting on God's word, even when your emotions desire to rebel and the thought process doubts.

The principle of God leading

The ark, which represented Gods presence, was a part of the procession around Jericho. It indicates God should lead in the destruction of a stronghold. God had taught Israel the ark was His presence among the people. The focus for Israel was to keep their eyes on the ark, not on the walls. So it is with believers. They must focus on God, not on the stronghold. If a stronghold is to be destroyed, a believer should keep his eyes focused on God and not on the problem. God is the Lord of every problem. If smoking is the stronghold, as long as you think about smoking you will be defeated and wind up smoking. However, if a focus is placed on the Lord, smoking can be defeated. Chapter three, exhortation on renewing the mind, will aid in refocusing the mind. A Jericho is not destroyed without the power and presence of God. A believer does not stand in his strength but in the Lord's. Paul wrote, *"Finally be strong in the Lord, and in the strength of His might."* Ephesians 6:10.

When a believer gives his or her life to the Lord it belongs to Him. The overcoming of strongholds is the Lord's problem. There is a song which states, "take your burdens to the Lord and leave them there." Most believers will shoulder the burden of defeating their stronghold without God's assistance. Actually it is His problem; His solution. When David went to battle, he said to Goliath, *"that all this assembly may know that the Lord does not deliver by sword or by spear; for the battle is the Lord's and He will give you into our hands."* This is the approach Christians should take toward a stronghold. God will deliver.

The principle of silence

Note the command Joshua gave to Israel, *"Joshua commanded the people, saying, 'You shall not shout nor let your voice be heard, not let a word proceed out of your mouth, until the day I tell you, shout! Then you will shout!'"* Why did God command them to be silent? One reason it eliminated boastfulness, which roots into pride. God wanted their hearts to be pure and for them to know victory came from obeying the Lord, not by their striking fear in the hearts of those in Jericho by their words. When one brags about a stronghold's destruction, prior to its destruction, it provides the evil one with an opportunity to test the believer in the area of his testimony.

Over the years I have seen people boast about being set free from a habit, only to discover the hold on them had not been broken. It usually made them want to withdraw from fellowship with other believers. On the eve of Jesus crucifixion, Peter violated this principle when he said, *"Even if I have to die with You, I will not deny You."* Jesus responded by saying, *"Simon, Simon, behold Satan has demanded permission to sift you like wheat."* Luke 22:31. When a believer, in the flesh arrogantly avows victory, Satan can immediately demand to test the believer in the area of his testimony. Peter lost the battle and so will believers if they rely on the flesh. Christians must wait on the Lord to bring victory. Do not allow pride to prematurely declare it. Do not announce any battle plans to the enemy. It is not boastful talking, which destroys strongholds, but an act of faith in God's strength and power.

The principle of shouting

The day came when a shout was necessary. It was a shout of faith. The people shouted victory before the walls fell, in order that it would fall. In destroying strongholds, there is still needed a shout of faith or an act of faith. This shout of faith was an open declaration of victory so that God would act on their behalf. It is saying I believe it is done. A shout of faith knows that God's plan was carried out to the letter, and then acting on faith declaring the stronghold's power and influence is being destroyed. Remember, faith believes something is so, before it is so, in order that it may be so. The time of declaring by faith the stronghold is defeated should originate with God, rather than from the flesh. Again allow me to remind you, I have observed people testifying as to a besetting sin as destroyed only to see them fall because of their boastfulness.

The principle of scripture or God's word

Not found in this passage in Joshua is the citing of God's word. However, Jesus refuted Satan's attack by quoting scripture. He said to Satan, *"Man shall not live by bread alone, but on every word that proceeds out of the mouth of the God."* Joshua did not have the privilege of having the written word of God as do present day believers. How much more should we Christians use God's word to defeat our strongholds? Remember a stronghold may be in the flesh, but **the powers of evil** or the Goliaths are ready to stand against the believer. Paul wrote to the Church in Ephesus, about standing in the strength of the Lord. He encouraged believers to put on the whole armor of God. This will be discussed in the following chapter. The only offensive weapon is *"the* *sword of the Spirit, which is the word of God."* Ephesians 6:17. The Greek word for "word" used in Ephesians is not the written, but the spoken word of God. The nation of Israel was acting on God's word. The word of God contains the purpose and promises of God about a matter. He desires the believer to be free from Satan and sin. When the day comes for its defeat, use the word of God against it. One of the best ways to utter a warfare prayer is to find a passage from the word of God and pray aloud the promise.

The principle of participation

The Bible records all of the people participated, *"So the people went up into the city, every man straight ahead, and they took the city."* Joshua 6:20. When a church faces a Jericho, the church needs to be united in waging warfare. Often if not most of the time, when a major problem arises in a church, instead of jointly attacking the problem Christians chooses sides. Most of the time neither group is in the will of God and He is not on either side. When a church faces a severe challenge it is imperative to seek the mind of God. Jericho's can only be defeated with God's help. Many times a church will not know the presence and work of the forces of evil in the problem. In a church believers are not to be spectators but must be warriors. In the same manner, the family may have a stronghold to defeat and it needs to be a combined spiritual effort in its destruction.

The Resolve in a Stronghold's Destruction

IT WAS TO BE UTTERLY DESTROYED

God's command through Joshua was, *"Keep yourselves from the things under the ban, lest you covet them and take some of the things under the ban, so you would make the camp of Israel accursed and bring trouble on it."* The destruction of Jericho had a warning. God told Joshua everything in the city belonged to Him. He promised a violation of the ban would bring trouble. Everyone except Rahab's household was to be destroyed. Achan coveted some of the money of Jericho and paid the price for his sin. Read about the results of Achan's covetousness in Joshua 7:1-26.

The principle is to see a Jericho or stronghold as wicked and evil and everything in it as belonging to God. Nothing is to be retained for oneself. To covet some aspect of a Jericho is to invite personal defeat. Covetousness itself can be a stronghold. Strongholds are compounded sin with demonic oppression. You cannot destroy sin and resist Satan and attempt to exploit the stronghold at the same time. Resentment and anger will find root into the same stronghold. The root is usually pride. One cannot say, I will confess my problem with anger, but I refuse to forgive the horrible sin done to me, and expect a stronghold to be destroyed. No part of a stronghold should be a sacred cow that cannot be touched. The attitude must be "Lord, what ever it takes, that is my desire." Remember, any known stronghold is anti God. It must be seen as evil. It must be utterly destroyed. In its destruction the way is paved to have victory over life. Jesus said, "*The thief (Satan) comes only to steal, and kill, and destroy; I came that they might have life, and might have it abundantly.*" John 10:10. The abundant life is here on earth. It is His desire for the believer to be victorious in destroying strongholds.

IT WAS NEVER TO BE REBUILT

"*Then Joshua made them take an oath at that time, saying, Cursed is the man who rises up and builds this city Jericho with the loss of his first born he shall lay its foundation, and with the loss of his youngest son he shall set up its gates.*" Joshua 6:26. The city was so wicked, God allowed a curse to be placed upon it. He did not wish for it to remain and contaminate Israel's spiritual walk. The believer should see his or her stronghold in the same way. Once it is destroyed, never permit it to be rebuilt. It should be seen as utterly wicked. In regard to the believer's walk the stronghold should be viewed as Israel regarded Jericho. This requires a determination and commitment when freedom comes never to be enslaved by the same sin problem. It is to be continuously on the alert to a sin's building blocks, which compose a stronghold. The Lord supported the curse. He allowed it to happen to Hiel the Bethelite who lost his oldest and youngest sons. 1 Kings 16:34.

The elevator Christian life is a result of a shallow confession. Christians who want instant cleansing usually confess those sins open to the conscious mind. However, numerous unconfessed sins abound in the subconscious mind. Soon, the subconscious drags a Christian back into sinful acts; thus, an elevator Christian life. A Christian must confess away and ask for cleansing for sinful acts, which God can bring to the mind that were committed years ago. One may say, "I can't remember those sins." Paul stated that *"we are divinely powerful"* and *"we are taking every thought captive to the obedience of Christ."* Under the power of the Holy Spirit, God will bring into conscious reality sins on which strongholds are built. These sin strongholds are found in the subconscious mind. Confessing away this stronghold's influence is replacing in the mind a positive element of grace, love and mercy to previously committed sin. These sins may have been forgiven in the past, but are logged in the mind and therefore retain power over the believer. A believers prayer is to break the power which is part of the stronghold and take away any ground the forces of evil have in influencing the stronghold.

This is the application of Romans 12:1-2. Paul wrote, *"I urge you, therefore, brethren, by the mercies of God, to present your bodies a living and holy sacrifice, acceptable to God, which is your spiritual service of worship. And do not be conformed to this world, but be transformed by* **the renewing of your mind**, *that you may prove what the will of God is..."* The mind is the storehouse for strongholds. The renewal of the mind is a must if they are to be destroyed. If this was not accomplished in chapter three return and deal with the past.

Verbal Commitment to the Lord

I know every Christian faces a Jericho in life. I am willing for You to show me the Jericho, which needs to be destroyed in my life. I will follow Your leadership in its destruction. I recognize that Paul wrote, *"For though we walk in the flesh, we do not war according to the flesh, for the weapons of our warfare are not of the flesh, but divinely powerful for the destruction of fortresses."* 2 Corinthians 10:3-4. Under the leadership of the Holy Spirit, You can bring into conscious reality sins on which strongholds are built. Strongholds are based in the mind. I realize I must destroy some of the stronghold's power through the confession of prior acts and attitudes of sin in the realm of the stronghold. I know God has forgiven me of those sins. However, confession is needed to destroy the power of the stronghold on the conscious and unconscious mind. I remember we were encouraged in Session 2 to follow the admonition of Paul. He wrote, *"I urge you, therefore, brethren, by the mercies of God, to present your bodies a living and holy sacrifice, acceptable to God, which is your spiritual service of worship. And do not be conformed to this world, but be **transformed by the renewing of your mind**, that you may prove what the will of God is..."* I am joining the process of renewing the mind.

Thought Provoking Questions

1. What strongholds do you see in the lives of your friends or family, which impede their growth in the Lord? Is there anyway you can help them destroy their stronghold?

2. How does a stronghold aid the evil powers in waging war against a believer?

3. If you had the tendency to develop a stronghold, on the level of the emotions, what would it be? What can be done so that it never becomes a stronghold?

4. Do you think a person who is in Bible study and church on a regular basis can have a stronghold?

5. Can a Christian be filled with the Spirit and have a stronghold?

6. In your opinion, what constitutes a stronghold?

† Warfare Prayer

Father, I confess I have a stronghold of (name your stronghold). Father, it took the children of Israel 40 years before they were ready to attack their stronghold, which was Jericho or unbelief. Before the attack they submitted to the rite of circumcision. This showed their love and commitment to You. I want to endorse Romans 12:1-2. It is my desire to be in total submission to Your leadership. I willingly apply the above principles in attacking my stronghold. I realize my stronghold is an area which allows me to be vulnerable to the attack of the evil one. I commit myself to You, and I am willing to pay any cost for the stronghold's destruction. Since this stronghold is on the level of the soul, I am willing to confess all sin connected to it, or which is influencing it. By faith, I accept its destruction before it is destroyed, in order that it may be destroyed. I rejoice in victory over the destruction of my stronghold. I ask You to remove and delete the power behind the stronghold and give me inner peace.

STEPS OF ACTION

- Determine the nature of your stronghold. Ask yourself a series of questions which will help ascertain its root and strength. These questions may include the following: How long have I had this problem and when was the first time it occurred? Is this problem virtually uncontrollable? If I asked those who know me best, "What is my greatest weakness?" What would they say?

- Ask God to bring to your conscious mind past incidents in which the stronghold expressed its control. Write down anything, which comes to your mind and is confirmed by the Holy Spirit. After you have finished writing, go over each thing asking the Lord to cleanse your mind and soul and to destroy the power behind the acts, attitudes and thoughts. Writing down helps you to remember and in future time keeps you from allowing Satan to condemn you for past and forgiven sins. Confessing sins, which God has previously forgiven, is building up a stronghold of unbelief.

- No matter what others may do, leave nothing undone on your part. Confession of sin is necessary for fellowship with God and the destruction of strongholds. Continue at this for as long as it takes to get victory. Victory is having an inner peace and relationship with God. It's knowing in your spirit that sin no longer has mastery over you. In Christ every believer is free from the power of sin. So destroying strongholds is realizing your freedom from the power of sin. Remember it may take weeks to completely destroy the power of sin found in the subconscious mind.

- Remind yourself that this is a walk of faith. Memorize a scripture, which illustrates the power of God. An example is: "...*and what is the surpassing greatness of His power to us who believe... which He brought about in Christ, when He raised him from the dead, and seated Him at the right hand in the heavenly places, far above all rule and authority and power and dominion, and every name that is named, not only in this age but also in the one to come. And He put all things in subjection under His feet, and gave Him as head over all things to the church.*" Ephesians 1:19-22.

- Once the stronghold is destroyed do not allow it to be rebuilt. Resist those things, which make up the stronghold. The area in which a believer is most vulnerable is the weakness of a stronghold.

Chapter 13

❧

Preparation for Spiritual Warfare
Ephesians 6:10-17

The following are a few questions, which need to be answered before a believer begins this study. Be honest and answer each question without attempting to determine what God would have you write.

1. What is spiritual warfare?

2. Are Christians immune to an attack on the level of the mind, will and emotions from demons?

3. Can the forces of wickedness cause health problems?

4. What can be done to thwart the attack of demonic forces?

Introduction

This exposition is purposely placed, in order for Christians to be prepared spiritually to engage the enemy in spiritual warfare. In the process of controlling the emotions, one often encounters the powers of darkness. Satan can attack the body, causing it to malfunction, although most of the demonic attacks come through the mind and emotions. As a believer learns to control the emotions he is ready to take up an offensive position. In this passage Paul did not refer to the emotions or the mind, but he does indicate that warfare is not against flesh and blood.

As had been noted before, this warfare is recorded in 2 Corinthians 10:3-4. He wrote, *"For though we walk in the flesh, we do not war according to the flesh, for the weapons of our warfare are not of the flesh, but divinely powerful for the destruction of fortresses."* A believer is at war with the demonic, as was Jesus. This is noted in I John 3:8:*"The Son of God appeared for this purpose, that He might destroy the work of the devil."* The great intercessory prayer of Jesus, prior to His crucifixion, was to protect the disciples from the devil. Note how His prayer involved spiritual warfare, *"I do not ask Thee to take them out of the world, but to keep them from the evil one."* John 17:15. In the model prayer Jesus taught the disciples to pray, *"... and deliver us from the evil one."* Matthew 6:13. Evil one is translated evil in most bibles; however, the accurate translation is evil one. One of Satan's schemes is to convince believers they are not in a fight. He persuades them believers are basically immune to attack and spiritual warfare is a bunch of hogwash. Since Jesus came to destroy the works of the devil, believers should investigate the nature of spiritual warfare.

> **Text:** *"Finally, be strong in the Lord, and in the strength of His might. Put on the full armor of God, that you may be able to stand firm against the schemes of the devil. For our struggle is not against flesh and blood, but against the world forces of this darkness, against the spiritual forces of wickedness in the heavenly places. Therefore, take up the full armor of God, that you may be able to resist in the evil day, and having done everything to stand firm. Stand firm therefore, having girded your loins with truth, and having put on the breastplate of righteousness, and having shod your feet with the preparation of peace; in addition to all, taking up the shield of faith with which you will be able to extinguish all the flaming missiles of the evil one. And take the helmet of salvation, and the sword of the Spirit, which is the word of God."*

The Strength for Victory

STRENGTH THROUGH A RELATIONSHIP

The command for strength

The Lord through the apostle Paul commanded believers to stand in the strength and power of the Lord. He wrote, *"Finally be strong in the Lord."* Be strong means to empower, to be strengthened. It is a present passive imperative. This command, to be strong, has continuous action. It indicates a continuous or daily effort of being strong in the Lord. The idea is to clothe oneself with strength as one would put on a shirt or other apparel. This is specifically seen in verse eleven. Paul could have said, be strong in the strength of your might, but this would have been untrue. When a believer encounters the spiritual forces of wickedness, he realizes the need for supernatural strength. If a Christian was warring with flesh and blood, he might not need the strength of the Lord. When the weapons of warfare are not of the flesh, they are spiritual. The command is for spiritual strength to fight a spiritual battle. Remember, the attack will probably come on the level of the soul. Jesus defeated Satan, and the need is for His strength. No believer has ever defeated Satan without employing the strength of the Lord.

The context of strength

Believers are commanded to be strong *"in the Lord."* "In the Lord" indicates the strength is in the realm or sphere of the Lord. This strength is derived from the Lord. He expands this thought by describing it as *"in the strength of His might."* "Strength" means relative or manifested power. It usually denotes the presence of strength rather than the exercise of strength. This word in the Greek always refers to the strength of the Lord. It is the overwhelming greatness of God's power. This power, might or strength is demonstrated in and through believers. It is the supremacy of God's strength over the forces of evil. The second word *might*, has the meaning might, strength, or power. It is the ability to produce results through power that is inherent in Him. This speaks of God's ability to perform as God.

This is the basis on which He established His church and "... the gates of hell shall not overpower it." Matthew 16:18. Gates are defensive, not offensive equipment. Hell cannot stand against God's might and power through the church. Paul indicated the church had responsibility to reveal God's might to the demonic world. He wrote *"In order that the manifested wisdom of God might now be made known through the church to the rulers and the authorities in the heavenly places."* Ephesians 3:10. The victory through the cross and in the resurrection was to provide believers with the ability to resist the demonic forces of darkness. Paul said, *"For the weapons of our warfare are not of the flesh, but are divinely powerful."* 2 Corinthians 10:4. In order to resist in the evil day a believer should have applied the previous expositions in every day living.

STRENGTH FOR VICTORY THROUGH RIGHTEOUSNESS

The command for godly armor

Paul gives a command to put on godly armor, *"Put on the full armor of God."* The Greek word "put on," means to put on or to clothe oneself. It is an aorist middle imperative. It is a command, which calls for a committed action. To put on the whole armor is a completed act. It is not done gradually but all at one time. "Full armor" is a combination of two words and literally means all weapons. The Greeks used it to describe the complete equipment used by the soldiers. Paul's idea for the believer, in this warfare against evil, was to prepare oneself fully and completely, as a soldier prepares for battle. I believe the putting on of the full armor is a daily life where the Lord is in charge. It is being filled with the Spirit or walking daily in the Spirit and not in the flesh.

The constitution of godly armor

Armor of God describes the spiritual makeup of God's character. Paul describes this in 2 Corinthians 6:6-7, "... *in purity, in knowledge, in patience, in kindness, in the Holy Spirit, in genuine love, in the word of truth, in the Power of God, by the weapons of righteousness for the right hand and the left."* Also Paul wrote a similar message to the Roman believers, *"The night is almost gone, and the day is at hand. Let us therefore lay aside the deeds of darkness and put on the armor of light."* Romans 13:12. The armor is described in more detail in verses 6:14-17. The description of the armor describes the Person of God. *Put on* is in the middle voice and means to place the armor upon oneself. This is literally putting Christ on oneself. Paul used this word, put on in Romans 13:14, *"But put on the Lord Jesus Christ, and make no provision for the flesh in regard to its lusts."* The articles of armor that are to be put on will be described later in this exposition. By looking at these verses one readily sees that <u>the armor is nothing more than the character of God.</u> God's fighting equipment is the nature of His Person. Satan's fighting equipment is the nature of his person. Believers cannot fight Satan with lies, deceit, resentment, hatred, anger, lust, or any of the deeds of the flesh. They must use the armament of God.

The Stand of Victory

THE RECOGNIZED SCHEMES

Paul wrote that standing firm was *"against the schemes of the devil."* "Scheme" denotes craft, deceit, a cunning device or a wile. It conveys the idea of scheming and craftiness. Paul wrote to the Corinthians regarding the ability of Satan's craftiness, *"But whom you forgive anything, I forgive also; ... in order that no advantage be taken of us by Satan; for we are not ignorant of his schemes."* 2 Corinthians 2:10-11. The word for "schemes" means thoughts, or that which is thought out. Satan and his evil cohorts are continually thinking of ways to attack believers.

The reason for putting on the armor of God is, *"that you may be able to stand firm."* "Stand firm" indicates not having to give ground when attacked by the enemy. The only way to stand firm is to put on the whole armor of God. The other side of the question is, "Can the devil be resisted through man's strength or ability without God?" Stand indicates steadfastness. Stand is used in this context to invoke a picture of a guard at his post or a soldier holding an assigned position on a battlefield. As a soldier is expected to stand in preparation for battle, so a believer is to be prepared for any attack. A believer, to be effective, must be willing to engage the enemy. I have heard many Christians say, "I do not want anything to do with spiritual warfare." Any statement like this concedes victory to Satan. They are unwilling to stand and somehow believe if they do not stand there will not be a fight. There is no such thing as being a Christian and not having to engage in spiritual warfare. Believers are in a fight, even if they do not fight. **The stand of a Christian is not requested, but demanded.**

THE RECOGNIZED STRUGGLES

The nature of the opposition

Paul uses the word *struggle*. "Struggle" refers to hand to hand fighting or wrestling. Thayer says it is, "a control between two in which each endeavors to throw the other, and which is decided when the victor is able to press and hold down his prostrate antagonist, namely, hold him down with his hand upon his neck." It is thought that the loser in a Greek wrestling match had his eyes gouged out and it resulted in blindness. If this were true it would create an emotional reaction on behalf of the believers in Ephesus. It communicated loud and clear to the Ephesians the seriousness of the struggle against the forces of evil. Jesus said of the devil, *"The thief comes only to steal, and kill, and destroy."* John 10:10.

Satan attacks God through His children, so it behooves believers to be aware of the wicked one's nature. Jesus in speaking to the Pharisees said of the devil, *"You are of your father the devil, and you want to do the desires of your father. He was a murderer from the beginning, and does not stand in truth, because there is no truth in him. When he speaks a lie, he speaks from his own nature; for he is a liar, and the father of lies."* John 8:44.

No matter how much a believer would like to ignore the devil, it is impossible. He invades every fabric of life through the evil that exists in the world. No matter how much Christians would like to ignore the forces of evil, they are real. Pretending they do not exist is like an ostrich hiding its head in the sand. Ignoring the devil is not the answer, warfare is the answer.

The nature of the opponents

Paul lists four classes of spiritual opponents. There are varying degrees of interpretation about these forces of evil. They are described as rulers, powers, and world forces of this darkness and spiritual forces of wickedness in the heavenly places. "Rulers" are rulers or first ones.

Some have translated rulers as prominent ones. "Powers" is powers or authorities. Some scholars believe these are titles describing the leaders of demons and these terms reveal subordinate ranks of demons. "World forces of this darkness," in the singular are used to describe Satan. Here it probably means Satan and his demon forces. "The term spiritual forces of wickedness" are probably another way of describing the demon forces.

Paul used two of these terms in Colossians 2:15, "*When He disarmed the rulers and authorities, He made a public display of them, having triumphed over them through Him.*" Paul uses a pronoun, which means against, before each of these four classes of opponents. Since the fight is against rulers, against powers, against world forces of this darkness and against spiritual forces of wickedness, it lends credibility to these being ranks of demonic forces. It is unlikely that Satan having great intelligence would not delegate authority through organized channels. To let his demon forces run amok is unthinkable. It does show believers are in warfare against unseen enemies.

The above passage from Colossians 2:15 indicates Jesus has defeated these forces of evil. Paul wrote, "*He disarmed the rulers and authorities.*" One might say, "If they have been disarmed, how can they attack the believer?" The Lord has defeated Satan so believers can also be victorious. The final overthrow of Satan is still future. The disarming of the forces of wickedness provides believers with the power to resist the devil. This is why believers should, "*be strong in the Lord and in the strength of His might.*" Remember as an ostrich hides its head in the dirt pretending something doesn't exist, some believers also pretend there are no demons and they are not in a fight. Satan and his forces rejoice over being ignored. It frees them to attack and let the believer blame circumstances or even God for their evil work.

The Struggle in Victory

Spiritual attacks may be upon the body but are usually directed at the soul. The soul is mans mind, will and emotions. Paul uses the word "stand in" verses 11, 13 and 14. To stand firm requires an exercise of the will. Standing firm is in God's strength, with man's determination. The strength, power and armor of the Lord are of no avail without the **expended effort** of the believer. Victory in spiritual warfare is bringing

God into the fight with a resolute exercise of the will to be spiritually clothed. These articles of dress, described by Paul, are all spiritual. When a believer has an encounter with the powers of darkness, he should be clothed with the armor of light, rather than the armor of darkness. Some believers may believe they are dressed up in God's armor, when in reality they have on the armor of darkness.

This admonition by Paul came at the conclusion of some practical advice for every day Christian living. The failure to follow the advice found in Ephesians chapter four through six is to live contrary to God's will. James wrote, "*Therefore to one who knows the right thing to do, and does not do it, to him it is sin.*" James 4:17. Knowing God's will in a matter and rejecting it is in effect putting on the deeds of darkness. Paul said in his letter to Roman believers, "*The night is almost gone, and the day is at hand. Let us, therefore, lay aside the deeds of darkness and put on the armor of light... But put on the Lord Jesus Christ, and make no provision for the flesh in regard to its lusts.*" Romans 13:12,14. A believer must actively commit himself to spiritual warfare. I have heard many Christians indicate that they do not believe in spiritual warfare. This is stupid and is in violation of God's word.

Paul's admonition was, "*Therefore, take up the full armor of God, that you may be able to resist in the evil day, and having done everything, to stand firm. Stand firm therefore, having girded your loins with truth, and having put on the breastplate of righteousness, and having shod your feet with the preparation of the gospel of peace; in addition to all, taking up the shield of faith with which you will be able to extinguish all the flaming missiles of the evil one And take the helmet of salvation, and the sword of the Spirit, which is the word of God.*" Ephesians 6:13-17.

A COMMAND TO RESIST

Paul wrote, *take up the full armor of God.* "Take up" is an aorist imperative, which indicates an immediate and decisive action. This is a once for all decision. It is not to be made every day. Some religious leaders teach a believer should dress up in armor every day. These participles describing the putting on of the armor are all in the aorist not in the present tense. The aorist indicates a definite and decisive act of taking up the armor of God. This act of taking up the armor of God is getting prepared for battle. This is a **command and should be obeyed.** It is a decision to resist, to engage in warfare. Paul wrote, *"that you may be able to resist."* *Able* means to be able, to have power or ability. Paul believed the only defense against the powers of darkness was the strength and armor of God. A believer can effectively resist the evil one in the Lord but not in his or her own strength. "Resist" is a combination of two words against and stand. This is an encouragement to be steadfast in your determination to resist the forces of evil.

The resistance is for a specific day. Paul did not say for an evil day or days, but **the evil day**. In the Greek, it is in the day, the evil. It is a particular day in which the believer is attacked. This day is characterized by the word evil, which denotes evil that causes labor, pain, sorrow, malignant evil. Wuest states it is "evil in active opposition to the good." A believer may have many evil days during his life when he is attacked. Christians ignoring the possibility there will be a potential spiritual battle, is conceding victory to Satan before the attack comes. This certainly does not prove to be the perfect will of God found in Romans 12:2. Putting on God's armor and standing in His strength is to be prepared for that day whenever it comes.

It is like a soldier having been trained for battle, ready for an encounter with the enemy. The enemy will not tell the believer when an attack is coming. Paul concluded this passage by stating, *"be on the alert."* A believer should be prepared for the evil day for he does not know the day or the hour that it will come. A soldier who was asleep or negligent in his duty and allowed a sneak attack, which brought defeat and could have been avoided, would be at least admonished if not some other punishment.

Paul adds, *"...and having done everything to stand."* This phrase could be translated and all things having accomplished to stand. "Done" is a combination of two words the Greek word for down and to work something, to produce something, to accomplish by labor. Thus it signifies to work out, achieve, or effect by toil. This is the opposite of idleness or inactivity. It speaks of the effort, the ultimate accomplishment or the achieving of the desired results. It is an aorist middle participle, which indicates completion. Paul indicated a believer should do everything necessary in order to be prepared for battle. It appears most believers would like to do as little as possible in order to stand. This reveals a need for believers to be determined to do whatever is necessary for protection.

CONDITIONS FOR RESISTANCE

The condition requires a personal relationship

Each of these articles of spiritual armor such as truth uses an aorist middle participle to describe the action of putting on. This indicates a self-prompted act. Since they are aorist, it again speaks of a decisive and complete act. Standing in the strength of the Lord does not mean the believer has no responsibility. The believer must gird the loins with truth, put on the breastplate of righteousness, shod his feet with peace and take up the shield of faith. Remember it is not necessary to dress up each day. If this were the case, Paul would have used the present tense. We will briefly look at each of these spiritual pieces of armor.

Truth objectively signifies the reality lying at the basis of an appearance; the manifested, veritable essence of a matter. Truth subjectively is truth in sincerity and integrity of character. To be a liar is to be opposite of being truthful. Jesus spoke about the devil being a liar. *"You are of your father the devil, and you want to do the desires of your father He was a murderer from the beginning, and does not stand in the truth because there is no truth in him. Whenever he speaks from his own nature; for he is a liar, and the father of lies."* John 8:44. A failure to stand in truth is to be clothed in the armor of the devil. Fear of evil forces is not standing in truth.

Righteousness is the character or quality of being right. When a person is saved, he is clothed with the righteousness of Christ. He dose not stand before God clothed in self-righteousness. Examine the way Isaiah describes man's righteousness. *"All our righteous deeds are like a filthy garment."* Isaiah 64:6. However, since receiving Christ righteousness is a self-prompted decisive act, it means the acceptance for oneself, the righteousness of Christ. That would be an open admission of one's own unrighteousness and the acceptance of Christ's righteousness. This is a denial of self-righteousness. Paul wrote, *"Therefore having been justified by faith, we have peace with God through our Lord Jesus Christ."* Romans 5:1. Justified, means to be declared righteous. A believer is not righteous as a man. However in God's eyes, sins are forgiven and any Christian has the righteousness of Christ imputed and imparted to his account. It is a determination to allow Christ's righteousness to flow through the believer. It is becoming more Christ-like. Paul wrote to the church at

Corinth, "*He made Him who knew no sin to be sin on our behalf, that we might become the righteousness of God in Him.*" 2 Corinthians 5:21.

Having shod your feet with the gospel of peace is a picture of a Roman soldier whose sandals were studded with nails, like cleats to provide a firm footing. "Gospel" is the good news of Jesus Christ which brings peace to a sinful heart. "Peace" is the harmonious relationship between God and man. Paul said in Colossians 3:15, "*...and let the peace of Christ rule in your heart, to which indeed you were called in one body; and be thankful.*" Peace has a clarifier, Paul uses the word preparation. "Preparation" can also mean readiness and it also can mean firm footing. The gospel of peace is to be the firm footing of the believer. The believer's walk should be worthy of it and an example of it. The above passage cited from Romans 5:1 indicates a believer has an inner peace with God. The presence of this peace gives assurance that a believer is in right relationship with God.

Faith is described as a shield. The Roman shield of Paul's time was oblong, two and one half feet wide and four feet tall. It was large enough for the Roman soldier to cover most of his body, especially the vital organs. The shield protected the soldier from the flaming arrows of the enemy. Flaming missiles or darts were arrows dipped in pitch, set afire, and were intended to maim, not kill the soldier. Satan does not hold the power of life and death over believers. He does have the ability to put a Christian soldier on the sidelines, injured. These missiles are anything coming upon believers which would destroy their testimony, create undue emotional stress, stir up anxiety create fear, and bring spiritual defeat. **Faith comes from God not man**. Faith is the exercise of God's known will, knowing God will do it. It is difficult to stand in faith against the enemy, and doubt the enemy can be defeated. All faith comes from God, even the faith to become a Christian. Faith may be viewed as an act or a condition of your walk. Faith may be that daily fellowship with God. It may be the steadfastness of living a sacrificial life. This does not mean that doubts will not come. It does mean during the whole day a Christian places his life in the hands of God. Faith gives the believer the ability to destroy the flaming missiles of doubt and discouragement, which destroy faith.

Jesus said to the disciples, "*If you had faith like a mustard seed, you would say to this mulberry tree, be uprooted and be planted in the sea; and it would obey you.*" Luke 17:6. At another time Jesus said the disciples could move a mountain. Faith, contrary to what some media preachers proclaim, is not based on naming and claiming. It is based on receiving a word from God and acting on the word. Faith to believe comes from God. The shield of faith is hiding behind and fighting with the word of God.

It requires a personal reception

The next piece of armor is the *helmet of salvation*. Paul commanded believers to take the helmet. "Take" is an aorist middle imperative. Its meaning is to accept by a deliberate and ready reception what is offered. It may be translated take but more accurately receive. Thus it is to receive the helmet of salvation. Paul makes this a command, which differs, in his approach to the first four articles. This does not mean that a believer must be born again every day. Salvation is seen as a three-fold act, a past salvation which is regeneration and justification, a present salvation which is sanctification, and a future salvation which is glorification. Paul must be referring to present salvation that is sanctification. It is the victory obtained through Christ's death, which gives the believer victory. Paul describes this in Romans 6. A short excerpt states, "... *and having been freed from sin, you became slaves of righteousness ... so now present your members as slaves to righteousness, resulting in sanctification.*" Rom. 6:18-19. Sanctification is a result of a daily walk with God.

The same verb receive is applied to the *sword of the Spirit*. It is to be received with a deliberate and ready reception. Paul identifies the sword as *"the word of God."* Word is rhema, not logos. Rhema denotes that which is spoken or that which is uttered in speech or in writing. Paul indicates that during the time of battle, a believer is to recite the scripture which the Holy Spirit reveals. This requires previous memorization. In Jesus' encounter with the devil, He resisted all of Satan's thrusts with quotations from the Old Testament book of Deuteronomy. When Michael, the archangel, was in warfare with the devil, he used the authority of God's word. Note what is written in Jude, "...*did not dare pronounce against him a railing judgement, but said, 'The Lord rebuke you.'*" Jude 9. A believer does not have the authority to rebuke the devil, but he does have the authority to stand and resist in the authority of the Lord. Jesus death and resurrection grants this authority.

The writer of the book of Hebrews wrote this about the word of God, "*For the word of God is living and active and sharper than any two edged sword, and piercing as far as the division of soul and spirit, of both joints and marrow, and able to judge the thoughts and intentions of the heart.*" Hebrews 4:12. Never discount the power of God's word. When

Gabriel came to Mary the Bible states, *"For nothing will be impossible with God."* Luke 1:37. The Greek literally reads, because will not be impossible with the God every word. The word here is the spoken word not the written word. It could be translated, "No word of God is without power." Believers have the Word of God the Lord Jesus Christ and the Holy Spirit and have the power to overcome the evil one in the evil day.

The Solution for Victory

THE INSTRUMENT USED IN VICTORY

Paul wrote, *"With all prayer and petition pray at all times in the Spirit."* The Greek word for prayer indicates prayers to God in general. "Petition" is an entreaty, a supplication. It is always addressed to God and is specific prayer. "Pray" is a present participle with continuous action. Paul indicates by using the aorist in putting on the armor a decisive onetime act, this prepares believers to go on the offense, which is through prayer. In using the present tense he communicates a continuous prayer offensive against the forces of evil. A believer's prayer is to be *"in the Spirit."* This means in accord with the Holy Spirit's will. Since the Holy Spirit is God, it would mean in accord with God's will. **Offensive spiritual warfare is praying.**

Paul indicates prayers for the most part should be for others, *"...be on the alert with all perseverance and petitions for all the saints."* When one is clothed in God's armor, standing by faith in His strength, there is seldom a need to pray for oneself. Most attacks from the wicked one come upon the believer through other people. As recorded in Matthew Jesus spoke to the devil when speaking to Peter and said, *"Get behind Me, Satan! You are a stumbling block to Me, for you are not setting your mind on God's interest, but man's"* Matthew 16:23. If Christians have performed according to the standards set forth in the above verses, there is absolutely no reason to express a warefare prayer for themselves. All they have to do is resist. Most prayer warfare should be on behalf of others. If one finds himself under attack and desires to pray, ask God to reveal the weakness in the stand. Remember, a believer in a submissive relationship, all that is needed is to resist the devil and he will flee.

THE INSIGHT IN VICTORY

Paul wrote "*be on the alert*." "Alert" is a composition of two words to chase and sleep. It is to chase sleep. It means to be watchful, alert, attentive or vigilant. A believer is to be alert for the attack of the devil, but not knowing when it is coming. On Tuesday, prior to Jesus' crucifixion, He told His disciples, "*But keep on the alert at all times, praying in order that you may have strength to escape all these things that are about to take place.*" Luke 21:36. Alert is a present participle, which has continuous action. The requirement is to be constantly on the alert. "Perseverance" has the meaning of holding out. It is not giving up and laying aside God's armor but waiting with expectancy for an attack, which will come. It is showing a healthy respect for the enemy. It is being prepared for "the evil day." Jesus warned Peter and the disciples on the eve of His crucifixion to be on the alert. Before He went to pray He said, "*Pray that you may not enter into temptation.*" After He found the disciples sleeping He said, "*Why are you sleeping? Rise and pray that you may not enter into temptation.*" Luke 22:40, 46. The disciples failed to heed His warning and fell into the trap of the devil. The disciples' actions have been repeated many times. Christians are so consumed by the things of the world they sleep through the time they need to pray.

Real Life Illustration

A nineteen-year-old man came for counseling. He had attempted suicide a number of times. He testified that something evil was speaking to his mind. This man had become a believer years previously, but had not walked with God. He was into the drug scene and said that he could not stop. He wanted to be set free from the assault of the devil. He was told that he must confess sin and accept his position in Christ. His mother was not a believer and was apprehensive about this method of help. He spent three days confessing sin. On the fourth day he was totally free from the satanic attack. He regressed only one time since that day. He called me and I encouraged him to confess the sin and dress up in God's armor again. This occurred many years ago and the last time I heard from him he was studying for the ministry. Remember this was a Christian who allowed sin to give the forces of evil a place or location to attack. Remember what Paul wrote, *"Be angry, and yet do not sin, do not let the sun go down on your anger, and do not give the devil an opportunity."* Ephesians 4:26-27. In the Chapter on anger we told you the word "opportunity" was literally the word "place." This young man had given the devil a place in his life.

Verbal Commitment to the Lord

I commit myself to standing in the strength of the Lord. I realize this is following the commands of the Lord. I will commit to living a holy life, one that will be well pleasing to God. I recognize holy living is the defense against the fiery darts of the wicked one. This is putting on the armor of God and standing in His strength. I will also take up the sword of the Spirit, the spoken word of God. This will require me to know and use God's written word. I also commit myself to prayer. I realize all real prayer is warfare. I am in the battle for the souls of men and women and most of this will be done through prayer. I will also pray for the saints who I see are in warfare.

Thought Provoking Questions

1. What does it mean to "be strong in the Lord and the strength of His might?"

2. Do you believe believers are in daily conflict with the forces of evil? If so how?

3. In what ways are believers under attack with the flaming missiles of the devil?

4. Why did Paul use the picture of armor and how does it apply to the believer?

5. Do you believe that you will be attacked by the forces of evil in the coming week? If yes are you spiritually prepared?

---
† Warfare Prayer

Father as a completed act I have put on Your armor. I know this requires total submission to You. I invite the Holy Spirit to reveal to me anything in my life which needs to be confessed or changed. Now that I have confessed all known sin, I know I am standing in the strength of Your might. I am prepared to allow the Holy Spirit to strengthen me in the inner person to be able to resist the forces of evil. Since I am submitted to you, I can resist the devil and he must flee. I believe that Satan and his evil force can't defeat me. I acknowledge putting on Your armor does not make me immune to the attack of Satan, but it does protect me in the midst of the attack. Thank You for Your divine protection.

STEPS OF ACTION

- Claim your authority over Satan by virtue of your position with Christ. Your position is given by Paul in Ephesians 1:20-21, 2:6, and Colossians 2:13-15

- Decide to put on the armor of God as a one time final act. Each day restate your position.

- Memorize appropriate scripture so on an evil day, Satan or one of his demonic spirits can be resisted.

- Keep guard over your mind and thoughts. Refuse any entrance into your heart and mind, anything of a negative or critical nature. Do not allow anything that is impure, unkind, offensive, unjust, evil, slanderous or resentful to occupy your thoughts.

- Accept the authority granted through standing in His strength and begin praying against the forces of evil, and especially for those you see under attack.

Chapter 14

∽

The Final Battle Plan-prayer
Matthew 6:9-13 Ephesians 6:18

Introduction

The last chapter dealt with prayer to some degree. However, this chapter will be a more extensive exploration on prayer although it will not exhaust the subject. The world utilizes a term to describe the uneducated as functional illiterates. They live, work, and play in society. Most of these are forced to take menial jobs because of their disability. They are unable to take advantage of prosperity and freedom as those who are more educated. In the same sense many believers, are functionally illiterate in prayer. They are unable to grasp the depth of prayer, or the freedom it brings. Most people believe the power and the privileges of prayer are for the spiritually elite. Members desiring prayer for a loved one or a friend besiege Sunday after Sunday pastoral staff. They believe leadership has more clout with God than they have. This is absolutely false. Every Christian has the same Lord who loves and answers prayer in accord to His will. The Lord desires that every believer know how to pray and pray effectively. This is the reason for the model prayer.

> *Text: "And when you pray, you are not to be as the hypocrites; for they love to stand and pray in the synagogues and on the street corners, in order to be seen by men. Truly I say to you, they have their reward in full. But you, when you pray, go into your inner room, and when you have shut the door, pray to your Father who is in secret, and your Father who sees in secret will repay you. And when you are praying, do not use meaningless repetition, as the Gentiles do, for they*

suppose that they will be heard for their many words. Therefore do not be like them; for your Father knows what you need, before you ask Him. Pray, then, in this way, Our Father who art in heaven, hallowed be Thy name. Thy kingdom come. Thy will be done, on earth as it is in heaven. Give us this day our daily bread. And forgive us our debts, as we also have forgiven our debtors. And do not lead us into temptation, but deliver us from evil. For Thine is the kingdom, and the power, and the glory, forever. Amen." Matthew 6:5-15.

"With all prayer and petition pray at all times in the Spirit, and with this in view, be on the alert with all perseverance and petition for all the saints." Ephesians 6:18.

A Review of Prayer

PRAYERS WHICH GOD REJECTS

The above prayer is often described as the model prayer. It is a simple prayer given to the disciples to reveal praying from the heart. Jesus warned the disciples not to pray like the Pharisees, *"And when you pray, you are not to be as the hypocrites; for they love to stand and pray in the synagogues and on the street corners, in order to be seen by men. Truly, I say to you, they have their reward in full."* Matthew 6:5. It was also a warning not to pray like the Gentiles. He also said, *"And when you are praying, do not use meaningless repetition, as the Gentiles do, for they suppose that they will be heard for their many words."* Matthew 6:7. These two passages indicate the Father does not answer these type of prayers. Before looking at the kind of prayer God receives, it is necessary to briefly describe prayers that God rejects.

He rejects the prayers of the wicked

A president of the Southern Baptist Convention found himself out of favor with some religious denominations when he said, "God does not hear the prayers of the unrighteous." He was absolutely correct. The scriptures verify this truth, "*The sacrifice of the wicked is an abomination to the Lord, but the prayer of the upright is His delight.*" Proverbs 15:8. Another passage states, *The Lord is far from the wicked, but He hears the prayer of the righteous.*" Proverbs 15:29. Again in Proverbs there is further support for this position, "*He who turns away his ear from listening to the Lord even his prayer is an abomination.*" Proverbs 28:9. The prophet Isaiah wrote, "*So when you spread out your hands in prayer, I will hide My eyes from you, yes, even though you multiply prayers, I will not listen. Your hands are covered with blood.*" Isaiah 1:15.

Peter wrote in the New Testament, "*For the eyes of the Lord are upon the righteous, and His ears attend to their prayer, but the face of the Lord is against those who do evil.*" I Peter 3:12. These scriptures reveal that God rejects the prayers of the wicked. However, if the wicked would repent and turn from their wicked ways God would hear their prayers of repentance. Once repentance takes place God hears their prayers.

He rejects the prayers of a carnal Christian

God hears the prayers of believers who live ungodly lives, but will not grant their request. James wrote, "*You ask and do not receive because you ask with wrong motives, so that you may spend it on your pleasures.*" James 4:3. God is not interested in giving man his wants and desires, to prove His love. God denies carnal prayers because He does love. God practices tough love with the backslider. If God was forced to answer any prayer, prayed by any believer, He would be subject to man's whims. All prayer, to be answered must be within the realm of God's will and purpose. His will and purpose is to be submissive to His leadership especially when the Holy Spirit convicts of sin. Carinal prayer could include the following:

- The inability to be prayed through to inner peace

- The attempt to persuade God by confessing sin

- To force one's will on God

- To have a resentment of God by a repeatedly asking why

PRAYERS WHICH GOD RECOGNIZES

He recognizes prayers originating from the desires. Prayers from the desires usually originate from the mind or the will. Many television evangelists have stated passionately that "God doesn't want His children to be sick." They have also said, "God doesn't want His children to be poor." Scriptures are cited which will lead many believers to pray asking God to heal a disease or to gain money. God does hear these prayers but does not obligate Himself to answer all prayers. Most of these type prayers are asked based on presumptuous faith. One of the passages used by them is, *"But He was pierced through for our transgressions, He was crushed for our iniquities; the chastening for our well-being fell upon Him, and by His scourging we are healed."* Isaiah 53:5. The rationale is every believer received complete healing through the cross and the only thing keeping them from receiving it, is faith. God's sovereignty does not grant wholesale prayers with the only requirement having enough faith. Remember faith to believe God for anything including healing originates from God. Belief without a confirmation from God on most things is presuming on God. God uses adversity to bring the believer into conformity to His will. This concept would negate the sovereign will of God. The following are some of the characteristics of prayers from desires:

- They usually misapply scripture

- They usually claim a promise from the Bible

- They usually rationalize their desires

- They usually express a false faith

- They usually presume on God's will

- This does not explain all prayer from the level of the soul, but typifies them

PRAYERS WHICH GOD RECEIVES

Paul wrote to the church at Ephesus, "...*pray at all times in the Spirit.*" Ephesians 6:18. Since Paul cautioned the Ephesians to pray in the Spirit, it would indicate believers could pray without the leadership of God's Spirit, this would indicate God would not necessarily answer this kind of prayer. I believe the Spirit of the Lord will place a burden within a believer, on the level of the spirit. This is the Holy Spirit alerting the believer to God's will in a matter. As this prayer is express often the inner burden is lifted. At that point, the prayer has been answered. However, if the burden continues, continue praying until the burden is lifted and peace fills the inner person. This may take a matter of days or even weeks. Burdens arising from the Spirit should encourage a believer. It reveals a relationship with God and He wants the believer to be a part of His work and will. In my opinion there are two ways to pray in the Spirit. One is to pray with an unfruitful mind and the second is to pray with a fruitful mind.

Praying with an unfruitful mind

The following scriptures are the basis for this category of prayers, "*And in the same way the Spirit also helps our weakness; for we do not know how to pray as we should, but the Spirit Himself intercedes for us with groanings too deep for words.*" Romans 8:26. "*For if I pray in a tongue, my spirit prays, but my mind is unfruitful.*" 1 Corinthians 14:14. There is the ability through the Holy Spirit to pray for others. This happens infrequently in the lives of most believers. This is not the gift of an unknown tongue as espoused by some, which they say comes as a result of being baptized with the Holy Spirit. Paul said the mind would be unfruitful. This indicates the mind cannot understand or is not privy to the level of the Holy Spirit's intercession. It is possible that warfare is taking place and the Holy Spirit knows how to encounter the enemy.

Praying with a fruitful mind

Jesus showed that it was alright to pray about upcoming trials even if the will of God was known and it went contrary to the person's will. He told the disciples a number of times in the weeks preceding His crucifixion what God's will and purpose for His life. However, in the garden He prayed, "*My Father, if it is possible, let this cup pass from Me; yet not as I will but as Thou wilt.*" Matthew 26:39. Jesus prayed this same prayer three times. It was not a sin for Jesus to ask the Father for a possible change in purpose for His life. This gives the believer the encouragement to pray for something, which may be contrary to the known, will of God. However, the resolve should always be, not my will but Thine be done. Jesus taught in the model prayer that believers should pray for God's will to be done. This does not mean they have to concur emotionally with His will, but that they are willing to submit to His will. He said, "... *Thy kingdom come, Thy will be done on earth as it is in heaven.*" Matthew 6:10. Jesus emotionally did not concur with God's will or He would not have asked God to change it. Jesus did willfully submit to the will of the Father. True prayer is the willingness to accept God's will even if the emotions scream for another answer.

Another aspect of praying with a fruitful mind is to pray without knowing God's will. Most believers' prayers fall into this category. They may know generally what God wills, but not the specifics. A believer may know that it is God's will for unbelievers to be saved. However, as they pray for a particular lost relative, they may not have the assurance this person will be saved. Paul wrote, "*Be anxious for nothing, but in everything by prayer, and supplication with thanksgiving let your requests be made known to God.*" Philippians 4:6. A person should continue to pray about a matter until the Lord answers the prayer or the believer senses in his spirit to cease praying.

CHARACTERISTICS OF PRAYING IN THE SPIRIT

It requires a spiritual relationship

By using the model prayer look at some of these characteristics. It is imperative to believe Jesus taught how to pray in the Spirit. He began by addressing the Father. He said pray, "Our Father." This should remind Christians prayer involves a person, and a relationship. It is difficult to have a relationship with a post. By using the term, Father, it stresses sonship, love, submission and obedience. Jesus added the words, "... hallowed be Thy name." This attitude of regarding God as holy is to see oneself as unholy. "Hallowed" means to make holy. In praise the believer is obligated to make holy the name of the Lord. This is done through praise and worship. Holy is being separated from that which is unholy, which is the world. God is totally separated from the world. As believers praise the name and glorify His holy nature, it should be done as those separated from the world. Otherwise the prayer would be hypocritical.

It requires a submissive response

Jesus said, "Thy kingdom come, Thy will be done." This is acknowledging God's sovereignty over all things. The truth is God does have a plan for man and that He is in the process of bringing His will to completion. This also demands a believer develop a servant attitude. Jesus said, "...give us this day, our daily bread." The owner of a slave had the responsibility of providing food and clothing for the slave. God desires to take care of the needs of His children. He wants them to depend on Him. Submission from man's point of view will be addressed later in this exposition.

It is acknowledging God's strength

Jesus went a step further showing the need for depending on the Father for protection from the god of this world. He prayed, "...deliver us from the evil" Deliver means to rescue from, to preserve from, or deliver. The word for evil in the Greek is literally the evil one. Jesus, on the eve of His crucifixion, prayed for His disciples. He said, "*I do not ask Thee to take them out of the world, but to keep them from the evil one.*" John 17:15. Paul wrote in Ephesians 6:11 "*Put on the full armor of God, that you may be able to stand firm against the schemes of the devil.*" Two verses later in this chapter Paul wrote, "*Therefore, take up the full armor of God, that you may be able to resist in the evil day.*" Spiritual praying is placing your self in the hands of the Lord. It is submitting oneself to the Lord and resisting the devil so that he will flee from the believer. James 4:7.

PRAYING FROM MAN'S PERSPECTIVE

It is praying in accord to His will

Many promises on prayers are given in the scriptures and can be misinterpreted. One of these is, "*And whatever you ask in My name, that will I do, that the Father may be glorified in the Son. If you ask Me anything in My name, I will do it.*" I have heard pastors preach and teach according to this scripture all you have to do is to ask and you will receive. Of course they say the reason you did not receive was a lack of faith. What does it mean to pray in the name of Jesus? Does it mean believers can use in Jesus name, to close each prayer and therefore pray in His name? This is not the magic formula that a believer should use to receive an answer to prayer. Praying in the name of Jesus is praying in accord with His will. As mentioned earlier prayer should be in submission go God's will. Praying in Jesus name is to pray in accord with all that the name of the Person of Jesus stands for. It must be in agreement with God's purpose and His Person.

The attitude of Jesus should be the attitude of believers. Jesus said, *"My food is to do the will of Him who sent Me, and to accomplish His work."* John 4:34. In His prayer in the garden of Gethsemane, Jesus prayed, *"My Father, if it is possible, let this cup pass from Me; yet not as I will, but as Thou wilt."* Matthew 26:39. **Jesus could not act apart from God's will.** He had a will of His own or He would not have said, "...not as I will." Praying for the will of the Father in a matter requires total submission to the Father's will. As Jesus could not operate outside of the Father's will while He was on earth, neither can He or the Father do so in heaven. Simply saying in prayer for the Father's will be done is not enough. A believer must be sincere in expressing to the Father for His will to be done. Numerous times this pastor has heard people say, "I want nothing more than the Father's will to be done in this matter." Yet while they were making this statement it was evident that they were not sincere. A person's attitude and actions, when a request is denied reveals the acceptance of the Father's will.

It is praying in acceptance of His work

Every believer should adopt the attitude of Jesus in His approach to ministry. He said, *"My food is to do the will of Him who sent me, and to accomplish His work."* John 4:34. Jesus received inner fulfillment for accomplishing the purposes of the Father. This statement was made as a result of the disciples saying, *"Rabbi, eat."* Jesus had shared the gospel with a Samaritan woman and some villagers. The response was so gratifying it brought the following response. He said to them, *"I have food to eat that you do not know about."* Believers should also receive fulfillment from accomplishing the works of the Father. Jesus also said, *"Truly, truly, I say to you, the Son can do nothing of Himself, unless it is something He sees the Father doing, for whatever the Father does, these things the Son also does in like manner."* John 5:19. Jesus never performed a ministry or acted outside of God's divine will and purpose. Jesus never performed a miracle which was not in accord with the will of God. He gladly accepted the position of allowing the Father to call the shots. For believers to pray in the Father's will they must accept the work of God, no matter what it entails. By the way it may be witnessing.

Jesus set forth the method for accepting His work in John 14:10. He said, *"Do you not believe that I am in the Father, and the Father is in Me? The words that I say to you I do not speak on My own initiative, but the Father abiding in Me does His works."* Jesus indicated the key to answered prayer was belief. In the same teaching, three verses later Jesus said, *"And whatever you ask in My name, that I will do."* John 14:13. Praying in Jesus name is praying in the Father's name. Jesus and the Father are one. Jesus cannot act apart from the Father. Therefore, by faith a believer must pray for the perfect will of God, and bring the emotions into harmony with His will. The mind and the emotions can think of many reasons why the current problem is not the work of the Father. Faith agrees the Father can cause all things to work together for good. God operates according to certain laws or principles. Isaiah declares this truth, *"For My thoughts are not your thoughts, neither are your ways My ways, declares the Lord. For as the heavens are higher than the earth, so are My ways higher than your ways, and My thoughts, than your thoughts."* Isaiah 55:8-9. Christians should look at the trials of life from God's perspective and thus accept that God is working good though them.

It is praying in adherence to God's word

Jesus said, *"If you abide in Me, and My words abide in you, ask whatever you wish, and it shall be done for you."* John 15:7. Many Christians ask amiss in their prayers. Jesus did not say, "Whatever you desire, pray and I will grant it." Praying in the name of Jesus is praying in agreement with His Person. Jesus indicated that abiding in Him was a prerequisite. Abiding in His person is agreeing with His word, will and ways. It involves a living relationship. Jesus described the method of abiding in Him in John 15:10. *"If you keep My commandments, you will abide in My love; just as I have kept My Father's commandments, and abide in His love."* It is also a loving relationship. Jesus said, *"If anyone loves Me, he will keep My word, and My Father will love him, and We will come to him, and make Our abode with him."* John 14:23. The Bible is God's word. God will not answer any prayer that goes contrary to His word. Jesus will not answer prayer, which is contrary to His character. The word and the character of Jesus are the same. A church leader once told me that he believed it was God's will to divorce his wife and marry

217

another woman. He justified his intended actions by stating he was not a believer when he married the first time and that his marriage was not joined together by God. This lame excuse is typical of those wanting God and or man to place their stamp of approval on their worldly desires. All praying in the Spirit is spiritual warfare. Most believers pray with their emotions without knowing the mind of the Spirit.

Verbal Commitment to the Lord

Repeat the following to another person or to the Lord, I commit myself to a renewed relationship with the Lord. I desire to be filled with the Spirit. I am willing to confess any sin revealed to me by the Holy Spirit. I recognize that I am in spiritual warfare every time I pray under the leadership of the Holy Spirit. I want to learn more about how to pray. I recognize that You only answer prayers that are in accord with Your will, work and word. I desire to know more of the mind of God, that I might know Your will. In my future prayers, I am going to ask You to reveal to me how You want me to pray about a matter. Since believers are constantly under attack I would like to be more offensive minded in warfare praying. I would like for You to give me the spirit of discernment, so that I might recognize the work of the forces of evil in every day's affairs.

Thought Provoking Questions

1. Do you believe demonic forces are at work in your personal life, the life of your family, in other relationships, and in the life of the church? If so write down some of his schemes.

2. Write down something that is heavy on your inner spirit. This is the starting point of prayer. How does the Lord want you to pray about the matter?

3. Do you believe God hears your prayers? If so why does He? If He doesn't, why not?

4. Is there anything keeping you from abiding in the Lord?

† Warfare Prayer

The following are some examples of praying in the Spirit:

Prayer using 2 Corinthians 10:3-5 as the basis

Father, in the name and authority of the Lord Jesus Christ and on the basis of my relationship with Him, I ask you to destroy any wrong thinking and speculation which keeps (name a person whom the Lord has placed on your heart) from knowing you. (or serving you if that is the case). I don't know what the stronghold is but desire that it be torn down. I ask for discernment or a revelation about the stronghold so that I may pray more effectively. Whatever it takes to bring (name) to you, I am in accord with Your will. I do not like to see anyone suffer or bear hardship, However, if this is the only way to accomplish Your will I will thank You and not feel resentment for the way you handle things. Continue to place a burden on my spirit for (name) until the stronghold Satan is using is destroyed.

Prayer using Matthew 12:29; 16:19; 18:18 as the basis

Father, I feel impressed in my Spirit to engage in warfare prayer for (name the specific work of Satan or the name of a person or ministry). Father according to Your word, You gave us the authority to bind and loose things on the earth. On the basis of this authority, I ask You to bind up the works of the devil so (name) will be set (name) free. Whatever it takes to bring this about, I am in agreement with it. I would like You to release peace not turmoil. I want to release the Spirit of love and joy in the lives of (name of person or ministry). I realize that it is not by my might and power but by Your Spirit that this prayer can be answered. I choose to accept Your will in the matter no matter what.

Prayer using, 2 Corinthians 4:4 as the basis

Father, the enemy has blinded the eyes of (name of person) so that he cannot see the light of the gospel. It appears that the word has been sowed on hard ground and Satan has snatched it away. I pray that You would soften the heart of (name) so the word would take root. Whatever is standing in the way of (name) being brought closer to receiving the word I pray that You would take it out of the way. I ask the things that please and fulfill the desires would become bitter. Hedge up (name) way, so that turning to You is the only solution. I ask the Holy Spirit use whatever means necessary to bring light into darkness. I make myself available to assist in this good work.

Prayer using Ephesians 6:18; Romans 8:26 as the basis

Father, I confess, I don't know how to pray about (describe the inner burden or inner leading). I do not know how to intercede. I request that the Holy Spirit intercede about this burden or open my eyes and reveal to me how to pray. If there is anything in my life, which hinders my ability to understand or limit my ability to pray, I want it taken away. Whatever it takes to make me a person who knows and understands your will, I will it to be done in my life.

STEPS OF ACTION

- Analyze your prayers by reviewing how do I pray? Do I use the name of the Lord as nothing more than a period or a comma? If I prayed the Lord's prayer as printed below would it be an insult to the Lord? Resolve to change your prayer habits.

- Ask yourself these questions: Are my prayers self-centered? Do they focus on finding God's will? Are they based on emotional needs and desires? Do they glorify the Father? Am I praying any warfare prayers?

- Ask the Father to place burdens on your inner spirit, so that you can know the will and purpose of God.

- Ask am I submissive to God? Am I willing to obey His commands? Is there anything between me and the fellowship of the Holy Spirit? Am I clothed in the full and complete armor of God? One of the ways to measure your submission to the Lord is evaluate two items. Do you have resentment in your heart for another person? Do you give ten percent of your income to the Lord's work?

How some people pray using the model prayer format

Father, who art in heaven, *Lord,* hallowed be Thy name. *God,* Thy will be done, *Lord,* on earth as it in heaven. *Lord,* give us this day our daily bread. And *Lord* forgive us our debts, *Lord,* as we also have forgiven our debtors. And *Lord,* do not lead us into temptation, but *God* deliver us from evil. *God,* for thine is the kingdom, and the power, and the glory, forever. I ask this in the name of the *Lord.* Amen. How would you like it if some one used your name in this manner? Does this show reverence to God and does He answer this kind of praying.

As I have written this book under the leadership of the Holy Spirit, I have prayed that you will have been strengthened in the Lord. God is faithful in his promises and I encourage you to be faithful to Him.

I welcome you to contact me with your successes utilizing the principals of this book in controlling your mental, emotional, and spiritual life. God bless you in your Christian walk.

About the Author

***

John A. Jackson was born in Cleveland, Texas then moved to Rock Creek Community near Shawnee, Oklahoma. He was saved at 12 years of age in Rock Creek Baptist Church. He moved with his family to Abilene, Texas where he completed high school. He spent four years in the U.S. Air Force. He is a graduate of Hardin Simmons University, Abilene, Texas. John was 28 years old when he felt God calling him into ministry. He and his wife, Lena, relocated to California where John graduated from Golden Gate Baptist Theological Seminary in Mill Valley, California. They have three children, Randy, Rick & Sherry and eight grandchildren. John pastored in Reedley, Anaheim, Fairfield and Highland, California. He served as president of the California Baptist Convention for two years. He served nine years on the International Mission Board; two of those as vice chairman and two as chairman. Recently retired, John and Lena relocated to Forney, Texas where he currently does pulpit supply for various churches.

Printed in the United States
61939LVS00004B/130-141

9 781420 856224